# MAKING ARCHAEOLOGY HAPPEN

## DESIGN VERSUS DOGMA

FRONTISPIECE. Excavation at the World Heritage site of Wanar, southern Senegal, observed by local people and visitors from a wide range of countries. The excavation, directed by Luc Laporte, is a joint research and conservation project between the Cheik Anta Diop University in Dakar and the University of Rennes, France (*photo by the author*).

# MAKING ARCHAEOLOGY HAPPEN

## DESIGN VERSUS DOGMA

### MARTIN CARVER

Left Coast
Press Inc.

Walnut Creek, California

Left Coast Press is committed to preserving ancient forests and natural resources. We elected to print this title on 30% post consumer recycled paper, processed chlorine free. As a result, for this printing, we have saved:

3 Trees (40' tall and 6-8" diameter)
1 Million BTUs of Total Energy
235 Pounds of Greenhouse Gases
1,061 Gallons of Wastewater
68 Pounds of Solid Waste

Left Coast Press made this paper choice because our printer, Thomson-Shore, Inc., is a member of Green Press Initiative, a nonprofit program dedicated to supporting authors, publishers, and suppliers in their efforts to reduce their use of fiber obtained from endangered forests.

For more information, visit www.greenpressinitiative.org

Environmental impact estimates were made using the Environmental Defense Paper Calculator. For more information visit: www.papercalculator.org.

LEFT COAST PRESS, INC.
1630 North Main Street, #400
Walnut Creek, CA 94596

**Left Coast Press** Inc.   *www.LCoastPress.com*

ISBN  978-1-61132-024-4 hardcover
ISBN  978-1-61132-025-1 paperback
eISBN 978-1-61132-026-8

**Library of Congress Cataloging-in-Publication Data:**
Carver, M. O. H.
Making archaeology happen : design versus dogma / Martin Carver.
p. cm.
Includes bibliographical references and index.
ISBN 978-1-61132-024-4 (hardcover : alk. paper)
ISBN 978-1-61132-025-1 (pbk. : alk. paper) ISBN 978-1-61132-026-8 (ebook)
1.  Archaeology—Philosophy. 2.  Archaeology—Social aspects. 3.  Archaeology—Methodology.
4.  Archaeologists. 5.  Antiquities. 6.  Excavations (Archaeology)  I. Title.
   CC72.C375 2011
   930.1—dc23          2011025113

Printed in the United States of America

♾ The paper used in this publication meets the minimum requirements of American National Standard for Information Sciences—Permanence of Paper for Printed Library Materials, ANSI/NISO Z39.48–1992.

# CONTENTS

# LIST OF ILLUSTRATIONS

# LIST OF TABLES

# PREFACE

These essays result from a relatively sober rewrite of the Rhind Lectures for 2010. I am most grateful to the Society of Antiquaries of Scotland and everyone who came to hear them for their support at the time and after, especially Simon Gilmour, the organizer and director of the society.[1] Giving the Rhind Lectures is a testing ritual requiring the speaker—who is often of retirement age or beyond it—to deliver six one-hour consecutive lectures between Friday night and Sunday afternoon, punctuated by numerous dinners and parties in which the people of Edinburgh have a particular expertise. As you can imagine, there is some pressure on the speaker to remain alert and diverting—or at least to prevent the audience and himself from relapsing into a coma. And this can result in various exaggerations, errors, spurious allusions, and unworthy jokes at the expense of friends and sparring partners, some of which I have probably failed to eliminate entirely in the text that follows.

My choice of topic for the lectures was prompted by a wish to reflect on 30 years of field archaeology before an informed audience. The organizers also remembered that Mortimer Wheeler's influential *Archaeology from the Earth*, published in 1954, had emerged from his own Rhind Lectures, given more than half a century before. On that occasion, the great excavator reminisced over his previous 30 years in the field and produced something halfway between a manual and a sermon, enlivened by his own inimitable rhetoric. So in some ways this was not a bad moment to take stock, do something a bit similar, see how well the Wheeler adages have survived, and how many of his predictions came true. We will see that an enormous amount has changed.

Unlike Wheeler, however, I had already put some of my ideas on fieldwork into a textbook (*Archaeological Investigation*, 2009), which came out a few

---

[1] The lectures as given, complete with song and pictures, comments and asides, will be found free to view online at *http://www.socantscot.org/article.asp?aid=1086*.

9

months before the lectures were delivered. So the present book is not a manifesto about how excavation should be done. It is much more like a lunchtime chat at the site edge, or in the bar at the end of the day, intended mainly for those already in the profession. I know that many people will not share my diagnosis or prescription, because it doesn't look like the world where they practice. My experience is primarily British and western European. Nevertheless, I have tried to cast the net wide when searching for comparable experience in the field and have also tried to catch some of the best of what has been published in the last few years. My hope is that one or two pieces of polemic will strike a chord and that the performers of one kind of fieldwork will sympathize with the actions of others, as sketched in these numerous vignettes, even while they are muttering "not what I would have done."

I am grateful to many friends and colleagues on and off site at the Universities of Birmingham and York, and in the archaeological firms with which I have been most involved (Birmingham Archaeology and FAS-Heritage Ltd). I have also found the meetings of the European Association of Archaeologists and the Theoretical Archaeology Group stimulating, although I am bound to say that opportunities for grown-up discussion of field methods seem to be few and far between, wherever you go. My hope is that such a need will be increasingly served by the Methods section of *Antiquity*.

I especially delight in an opportunity to thank Cecily Spall, Sue Hirst, Catherine Hills, and Madeleine Hummler for all they taught me and made me see. Moreover, there are now four archaeologists in my immediate family, Madeleine, Emma, Jay, and Gevi, each engaged in a different branch of the profession and each with a different view of what our discipline is for and how it should be practiced. I am very happy to acknowledge their influence and thank them for much firsthand information, as well as for the diversity of their convictions.

For all that, I believe that archaeological practice has become unduly fossilized, and our procedures are unambitious, unquestioning, standardized, resigned to a low quality and wedded to default systems—the dogma of my title. That's the main reason for writing this book: archaeologists spend the least amount of time discussing the most important thing they do.

Ellerton, October 2010

# CHAPTER 1

# A VISIT TO

# THE ANCESTORS

I began my Rhind Lectures with a song, partly because it reminded me of life on archaeological excavations, where I have spent some of my happiest hours, and partly to generate an insouciant mood on a daunting occasion. The audience shifted in its chairs, refrained from humming along, and located itself somewhere between respectful, embarrassed, and baffled. Belted out to the tune of "The Battle Hymn of the Republic," the song begins: "He dug a hole a mile deep without a context plan" (three times)—"and he ain't going to dig no more," followed by the chorus "Archaeology is an art—it's not a science" (three times). The misdemeanors of this villain are recounted in numerous verses—for example: "He drank a bottle of whisky and interpreted the site"; and the words "art" and "science" in the chorus are swapped around each time with increasing force, culminating in a joyous shouting match in which little can be distinguished.

Dating back many decades, and probably originating in the back of a minibus on the way to some campsite, these sentiments were meant to signal a new generation of professional practice and practitioners. The old ways, with their air-headed volunteers and self-serving professors, were gone forever; there was to be a new dawn for historical science spearheaded by the stratigraphic unit. As with all revolutions, something got lost. . . ." Archaeology is an art—it's not a science" (or the other way round) epitomizes a trowel-eye view of the indoor hand-wringing of archaeological theory, the choice between storytelling and understanding, intuition and analysis, insight and proof. It has been with us for some time, so our first duty is to pay a visit to the ancestors and see what they made of the conundrum. Here is Alfred Kidder (1885–1963):

The details of archaeology are in themselves so interesting that it is fatally easy to become completely absorbed in them, and there is always the excuse that without close and accurate work one cannot arrive at trustworthy conclusions. . . . The result is that too often one arrives at no conclusions at all. It is quite as fatally easy to ignore detail (with the plausible excuse that the close worker cannot see the forest for the trees) and strike out blithely on the primrose path of speculation. (Kidder 1924, 137–138)

Overall this is good advice: doing archaeology demands both art and science—so deal with it: a scientific adventure in pursuit of a story, observation in harness with imagination, precision in record, persuasion in prose. As we will see, since Kidder's day archaeological investigation has become embedded in the society where it is practiced, so it is a now a social science as well. The task of the fieldworker is to reconcile these aspects, the factual, the imaginative, and the social, and because of them, or in spite of them, to make archaeology happen.

British archaeologists pay homage to A. L. F. Pitt-Rivers (1827–1900) as their first ancestor, and the father of archaeological science. Pitt-Rivers, not without a little whitewashing, claimed empirical purity: "Every detail should be recorded in the manner most conducive of reference. . . . it ought to be the chief object of an excavator to reduce his personal equation to a minimum" (Pitt-Rivers 1887, xvii). But his younger contemporary Flinders Petrie (1853–1942) quickly showed this to be impossible: "The old saying that a man finds what he looks for . . . is too true; it is at least true that he does not find anything that he does not look for. . . . To state every fact about everything found would be useless. It would be like a detective who would photograph and measure every man on London Bridge to search for a criminal" (Petrie 1904, 1, 49). The modern police force, aided by large computers and an indoor workforce, might find this a fairly normal approach—but one knows what he means.

Comparing these last two maxims, one can't help noticing that for us, it is Petrie that comes across as the modernist, aware that the personal equation is part of what drives the inquiry—eliminate it (or pretend to) and you can eliminate the business of archaeology altogether. Mortimer Wheeler praised Pitt-Rivers and installed him as a role model, but was hostile and dismissive about Petrie. Why was this? Petrie was a cultured person and intellectually close to Wheeler, in that he was driven by a historical agenda (predynastic Egypt). Although not a military man, he was a heroic fieldworker, just as much at home in the desert as any veteran of El Alamein. Pitt-Rivers was not especially cultured or even greatly interested in history or prehistory. He treated his excavations like agricultural projects with sermons thrown in. He was just as much an absentee director as Petrie, but it was Petrie that Wheeler picked on.

I met Wheeler only once—not long enough to have an argument with, but we were both born in Glasgow and had both served in the army, and so I feel the argument would have been a good one. Wheeler is associated with a number of strong opinions. He admired Pitt-Rivers, but perhaps this was because, as an ex-general, Pitt-Rivers outranked him. He denigrated Petrie, describing his brilliant *Methods and Aims* of 50 years earlier as "quirky" and took him to task for delegating his supervision of excavations, claiming that "my pen melts" as he thought of Petrie's absenting himself from the site (1954, 15); but at least Petrie was away engaged in fieldwork. Wheeler's lofty posture can be modified by what he practiced, as opposed to what he preached. Here is Noel Myres' recollection of Wheeler at Brecon Gaer in 1924: "Rik himself treated the excavation as the agreeable background to a fishing holiday. He would begin the day by directing Christopher [Hawkes] and myself of what we were to find, and then disappear in the direction of the river. In the evening he would return, not always overburdened with the trophies of the chase, listen to what we told him of the day's work on the dig and explain to us what he thought it meant" (Hawkes 1982, 90). Unabashed by his own cavalier approach, Wheeler went on to paint Petrie as part of a whole Near Eastern catastrophe, which had somehow evaded his own organizing baton. We shall have to take a look at this particular prejudice.

Wheeler advocated a box method of excavation—and adroitly managed to promote his system as the option of the open-minded. At the start of his Rhind Lectures, he famously said: "There is no right way of digging, but there are many wrong ways" (1954, 1). I have often heard archaeologists repeating this dictum to each other with evident satisfaction. It was a saying typical of a man regularly intoxicated by his own rhetoric, but unfortunately it means very little. If there are no right ways and many wrong ways, then the ones that aren't wrong aren't right either, leaving us where we were. Clearly, what he actually intended to say was: "There are many wrong ways of digging, some of them truly ghastly, especially Petrie's, and only one right way—mine. Now: read, mark, learn and inwardly digest." His conviction about his own methods was unwavering. In his attack on Ian Richmond in *Antiquity*, he took a swipe at "the drawings of the sections, [which] in spite of their delicate limning, fail singularly to conform to modern standards. They are of the obsolete 'Bersu' type in which pictorial smudgery was substituted for hard-headed analysis . . ." (Wheeler 1968;

Hawkes 1982, 354). Here is naked dogma of the kind which archaeology apparently craves—the "right way" and the "obsolete way" are paraded with approval and disdain, respectively. Wheeler, like many who admired him, prized authority over creativity. Perhaps this was prompted by his military rather than his archaeological experience, but, having shared both, I would say that in neither field does the authoritarian have an advantage over the ingenious. I would, however, agree that those were other days, in which strutting intolerance habitually attracted a large following. But why do we still value it now?

When his ego allowed him, Wheeler brought good things to archaeology, perhaps most importantly, in the present context, his emphasis on neatness—which was right on the button. It is undeniable that some excavations in western Asia, including Petrie's and Woolley's, had an air of chaos, with hundreds of workers moving in contrary directions across a wrecked mud-brick ruin and down into life-threatening chasms. In a famous propaganda picture in *Archaeology from the Earth*, Wheeler contrasted the good order and military discipline of his parade-ground boxes with this Middle Eastern mayhem. However, equally horrible is the groping jagged trench perpetrated at Caerleon by Victor Nash-Williams, whom Wheeler described in *Still Digging* as one of his outstanding pupils (1956, 68, 71; Carver 2009, fig. 2.1b).

Untidiness rightly makes excavators vulnerable to the criticism of others and is often the starting point (and sometimes the only point) of public disagreement on method. Most practitioners are aware of its importance: without meticulous standards of neatness, excavation is not only pointless, but misleading. Petrie believed this too, and said on page 2 of his 1904 book: "Spoiling the past has an acute moral wrong in it." But strangely, things have, if anything, got worse: the images we carry away from a visit to a commercial site, or a university research project today, from TV programs or from exposures on YouTube, are far from flattering; the site looks more like a quarry than a laboratory. We see rows of disheveled trenches framed by sprawling upcast, or bleak expanses of gravel with a few professionals hurrying earth into a bucket, or a Roman ruin populated by shouting students, surrounded by collapsed fencing. Weekly on television, we see gushing presenters posed before sites to make you blush. Wheeler was spared seeing the messy digs on the popular British TV series *Time Team*, which began in 1994, eighteen years after his death at the age of 86.

Digging neatly is not simply an aesthetic matter. Özti, the ice man, was discovered by chance in the high Alps and excavated with ski sticks, before he was taken belatedly and slowly into a more carefully managed investigation. He emerged from his first analysis as a player in a Bronze Age drama: a mountaineer, fleeing his enemies, shot down and left to freeze to death. He did seem to be carrying an enormous amount of kit, but no-one wanted to ruin the story, until this year at least, when a group of Italian scholars suggested that Özti could be interpreted as a furnished inhumation burial—with very different implications for the occupation of the Bronze Age Alps (Vanzetti et al. 2010). In retrospect, we can imagine a completely different archaeological project, consequent on the first glimpse of the corpse: a tent, lighting, heating, the gentle extrication of the materials, the micro-topographical mapping, and the detailed survey of the immediate area, all of which turned out to be crucial to the interpretation.

What actually makes the difference between a good excavation and a bad one—or is everything relative? If there is to be no quality control in our profession, then it doesn't matter much what we do, and archaeology is a private indulgence, tolerated briefly by those with money to make and a vague environmental or humanist conscience. But no-one who cares about human experience on the planet believes that what we do has no serious purpose. So it will be constructive to look analytically at "good" and "bad" fieldwork and ask a few hard questions about circumstances, money, and response. What makes a successful inquiry? Is it luck, a good organizer with a military moustache, a gifted team, or a way with words? Or are there other factors at work, factors we can control or adapt or enhance to raise our game in our own estimation and that of the public we serve?

## Method and Sentiment in Mesopotamia

As a first step on the quest, it might be worth paying a brief visit to the "land of archaeological sin," as Wheeler dubbed the Middle East, just to see whether there is something inherently culpable in the region. Of course, there are plenty of examples of extravagant grubbing out of antiquities—but this is not unique to that region; and where tombs are large and rich, there will be robbing on a scale to match.

On the positive side, let's remember Claudius Rich, diplomat and flute player, intelligently exploring the desert cultures at the beginning of the 19th century. Long before Layard pillaged Nineveh, or what he thought was Nineveh, or Schliemann trenched Troy, or what he thought was Troy, Rich visited Babylon and carried out the first evaluation—using a surface survey and the sections of old quarry pits to inspect strata (Rich 1816). Exceptionally, he stole nothing but concentrated on making a topographical model of the buried town. Babylon attracted pioneers: at the same place at the end of the same century, Robert Koldewey was carrying out well-organized area excavations on a huge scale for the Berlin Museum, managing his excavators in a troweling line (Koldewey 1914).

Contrary to today's popular axiom of the pillaging colonial, the principal objective of most 19th- and early 20th-century excavators was not the acquisition of antiquities, or even the exposure of a great monument, but understanding the historical sequence from its earliest years. These sequences, lest we forget, created most of prehistory before radiocarbon dating; it was a tremendous achievement, laboriously sequencing pottery and palaces, temples and towns—work that remains of permanent value, however much later corrected in detail. It also developed a rich web of collaborative method which may escape the sympathy of the skeptical modern student. Naturally, this kind of digging required deep and narrow areas and the carrying of much spoil many meters upward. The workforce was generally marshaled and ranked, divided into small team-like platoons, each led by a pickman, assisted by a spade man, and served by basket boys, carrying away the baskets of earth, otherwise *zembiles*. The procedure was determined by the stuff; it was hard, full of mud bricks, some broken, some still in situ. A pick was needed, but an intelligent pick, using accurate force. In 2009, these tools are still needed and still in use, as are the "basket" record sheets (Bowkett et al. 2009, figs. 5.4, 6.4). Clearly there are responses here, to do with the type of strata, that have remained valid.

In colonial times, the workforce was predominantly local and the directors predominantly imperial: British, French, German, Italian, or American. But cool operators like Leonard Woolley prized their local foremen—and encouraged the upwardly mobile through a graded pay structure (1920, 96–145). In fact, it is arguable that the workforce at Ur was less prone to complaint than the 21st-century British contract staff we encounter in Paul Everill's PhD thesis, *The Invisible Diggers* (2009)—of which more presently (p. 75).

Disaffection there was, of course, but it was endemic to the century, which those alive at the time could hardly escape. But in addition to the zeitgeist, there were deeper and more personal forces affecting excavation that we must cope with too. Max Mallowan's memoir (1977) describes in graphic detail the pleasures and excitements of exploring ancient Mesopotamia and does not disguise the fact that excavation can be an emotional business. As second in command at Ur, he was able to observe Leonard Woolley at first hand and to learn from his ability to find tombs with the assistance of the locals—who knew them rather well. He also observed at first hand the sensationally beautiful and irredeemably awkward Katherine Woolley. In his memoir he tiptoes over her reputation as over broken glass, but we are left in no doubt that she was exasperating, willful, and demanding, and Woolley was at her beck and call day and night. When Max himself wanted to get married, he resigned, deciding he would lose his job at Ur since Katherine would tolerate no other woman on the same site.

The woman Mallowan married was Agatha Christie, the celebrated queen of genteel crime whom he met when showing her round the excavations. Katherine was to appear in *Murder in Mesopotamia* (1936) thinly disguised as Louise Leidner, where she is described as charming, with a blonde Scandinavian fairness, with lovely violet eyes—but a dangerous woman who caused quarrels. She is duly murdered, to the author's evident satisfaction, with a list of suspects that included practically everyone on the dig—at least everyone who belonged to the murdering classes (the Europeans). To the amazement of all (except Hercule Poirot), the murderer is none other than the adoring Dr. Leidner, her long-suffering husband.

Agatha Christie continued helping on excavations and in the pot-shed long after she was rich and famous, and she wrote a particularly affectionate account of archaeology in *Come, Tell Me How You Live* (1946). The period, with its pipe smokers dividing the foreign spoils, is now a sitting target for student essays on the evils of colonialism; but one mustn't forget that these archaeologists were people too, lived in their own times, and had strong feelings for the past and a pastime that they knew well how to share at every social level. One passage in Mallowan's memoir describing his first encounter with Tell Jidle recalls the enchantment that so many of us feel when embarking on a new project, even in today's contract archaeology.

> I have rarely seen a more delectable and beautifully situated spot. It was a compact mound with steep slopes, standing to a height of 15 meters and it covered about four and a half acres in all. The top of the mound directly overlooked the crystalline blue waters of the river which were transparent right down to the bed and teeming with fish; the banks were lined with a few willow trees and the only presence of human occupation was a small house which belonged to a lonely miller who ground wheat and barley brought to him by people in this district. How devoutly I hoped that this mound would turn out to be a good one. We could have happily settled down here for several years. (1977, 156)

This first step into the deserted garden is something we can all relate to; so are the personal stresses of a dig community, the local economy, and the vicissitudes of strata. If we want to know why excavations look different from place to place, maybe we should be making fewer assumptions about excavator ignorance and looking harder at the circumstances and the soil. In my judgment, the archaeologists of the old Middle East were not intrinsically bad, either technically or morally; they operated as they did because they were applying the objectives of their day to the kind of strata they had to deal with, in the social context they encountered and joined.

## BOXES AND PITS

These matters will be pursued in the chapters that follow; but we still have some other questions to ask the ancestors: such as why did the shape of an excavation matter? (FIG. 1.1). Wheeler's "box system," one of the best known, was intended primarily for the greater control of an unskilled workforce, each exca-

FIGURE 1.1. Ancestral footsteps. Overhead photograph of Sutton Hoo showing the traces of six methods of excavation in the same place. (1): Vertical shaft dug in the center of Mound 2 in ca. 1600 (*left, center*); (2): trench cut through Mound 2 in 1860 (*left*); (3): trench cut through Mound 2 in 1938 (*left*); (4): box excavation on Mound 5 (*right*) in 1970; and (5): quadrant excavation on Mound 2 in 1988 (the "pastry-strips," *left*). The whole area exposed was investigated by horizon mapping and detailed excavation between 1984 and 1990 (*photo by the author*).

vator's downward itinerary being tracked by the sections on the walls of their box (FIG. 1.2; see also Chapter 4, p. 102). As everyone knows, Wheeler liked to see women in his boxes—thus doubling the pleasures of the chase. Twelve of the fourteen assistants listed in the acknowledgments in the Maiden Castle report were women (Wheeler 1943, 2; cf. Hawkes 1982, passim). Not everyone reads the situation in an unworthy manner. The modern-day website *archaeologyexpert.com* hails Wheeler as a pioneer feminist: "Ladies to the Rescue" it says: "Wheeler's box system was adopted out of his respect for women." "Respect" can be read many ways; perhaps "admiration" would be nearer the mark. But it is not for us to condemn the rewards of the unintended consequence.

In the context of archaeological method, fieldworkers are not encouraged to reveal the many affectionate connections their work brings. But perhaps they should—not in a salacious or boastful way, but as an acknowledgment of otherwise unspoken debt. In Wheeler's case, the names of Tessa Verney Wheeler, Kitty Richardson, Kathleen Kenyon, and Beatrice de Cardi spring to mind as thinkers and practitioners that will have molded him, not just the

FIGURE 1.2. Wheeler's box system as deployed to examine the entrance to the Iron Age hillfort at Maiden Castle, Dorset, England (Wheeler 1943; *courtesy of the Society of Antiquaries of London*).

other way round. Archaeologists often form couples, and every partnership we have, whether it amounts to one or several, is deeply influential (because equal) and, just as often, unrecognized. Perched on some heavenly vantage point, we could see ideas traveling between one person and another and from site to site, blossoming at times of closeness and stored away at times of parting. It is not amazing that men and women give each other so much, or that they forget they do. But perhaps we would learn more from the history of archaeology if it were blessed with a little less self-promotion and a little more romantic credit. In my contention, good ideas in archaeology come less from the Musings of the Great and more from the Network of Intimate Acquaintance.

## RISE OF THE SINGLE-MINDED

Among Wheeler's predictions for the future given at the end of his Rhind Lectures were the arrival of total excavation—"we need the careful uncovering of a whole cemetery"—and the demise of the test pit—"the age of the sondage is now in large measure past" (1954, 215). Total excavation was duly championed in the 1960s by Martin Biddle and Phil Barker, both inspired by the Danish innovations of Gudman Hatt and Axel Steensburg, and was successfully executed at a cemetery containing more than 2,000 burials by Catherine Hills at Spong Hill in Norfolk (Hills 1977, and continuing). Barker was appalled by the random cuttings that laced the Roman site of Wroxeter and declared himself the enemy of the trench (1977). He realized that they had been dug by researchers looking for sequence, in the manner of their colleagues in the Middle East, and he saw this as impatient, selfish, and damaging. A site should be taken apart as it was put together, layer by layer, stone by stone. Wanting to know something particular was no excuse for a particular mode of digging. Everything except large-scale stratigraphic area excavation was a shortcut, as wrong-headed as driving faster in order to get to a garage before you ran out of petrol.

The Barker doctrine aligned well with the contemporary "rescue" movement, for which a lengthy and meticulous dissection giving equal attention to every trace had many attractions. The new army of stratigraphic area-excavators marched boldly through England and made several attempts to cross the Channel. Impressionable young British students were told that there were few more sinister practices to be encountered on the continent than the German *Schnitt* method—the non-stratigraphic slicing of strata into arbitrary cubes, something that sounded not so much like a loss of one's senses as an irreversible loss of manhood—as in "I've opted for the Schnitt."

But this procedure too has its rationale (see Müller-Wille 1991). Like the box method, it may have started as a control mechanism, since in the postwar years large-scale rescue projects made use of prison labor. Or it may have had some of its roots in the fact that sites on the loess, for example, are not stratigraphically strong—layers are often invisible. But it also exercised a scientific principle that is less appreciated by those who do not use it. The *schnitt* method depends on horizontal and vertical surfaces meticulously cleaned and recorded exactly as they are, with or without visible layers. No-one makes anything up. It is for the analysts at a later date to reconnect this three-dimensional geometry into consecutive stratigraphic episodes. Thus its protagonists would maintain that, far from ignoring stratification, they are recording it more precisely and objectively, and in a manner that is checkable. For this reason, they reserve the right to remain unimpressed by a sequence created by individuals removing strata in single layers, pieces, or "contexts," a practice the British promote with an almost religious fervor.

The "single-context" method enjoyed a vogue in late 20th-century Britain, especially in towns and especially where there was sufficient money to employ a skilled—or at least a dedicated—workforce. The context itself was invented by Max Foster at York in 1972, as a general term for a stratigraphic unit, whether layer, interface, hole, or bunch of stones. Proforma recording, with each context on a separate sheet, was developed by Sue Hirst at Bordesley Abbey (Hirst 1976). The record was extended, notably by Steve Roskams at MoLAS (the Museum of London Archaeology Service), to include the pre-excavation plan of each context on a single sheet (thus "single-context planning") (see Roskams 2001, chap. 9). This made it easier to recall the order of deposition and, in some ways, answered the criticism of the *schnitters*, since the perimeter of a later context ought to be corroborated by the earlier. The order of deposition was represented on a stratification diagram, of which the most widely promoted version was the Harris matrix (Harris 1975; 1989). This represented the sequence as a number of boxes connected by horizontal and vertical lines. These two instruments—the definition of individual contexts and their placement in a sequence diagram—meant that many participants could dig and record independently and so contribute directly to the build-up of a large model of the total sequence. They could, in effect, feel they were acting like scientists putting together a giant jigsaw puzzle, the virtues of which were self-evident. Unfortunately, the single-context system, combined with area excavation, rapidly became another dogma, with the dogma's doleful corollary: *look no further*. The faithful are still on campaign; in 2004 Richard Greatorex reported breathlessly: "Archaeologists in both France and Belgium have now adopted the Harris matrix on their excavations. . . . Even though it might be too early to talk in terms of developing an official European Archaeological Recording System, use of the Harris Matrix appears to be growing in an increasing number of countries, and may eventually be adopted throughout the Continent" (Greatorex 2004, 268).

How strange, then, that for all this evangelical reverence, the package still remains confined to a rather narrow base, both ethnically (British), economically (well-funded), and typologically (urban excavations). What kind of insecurity, what fear of originality, drives people to preach such narrow prescriptions? It is one thing to swear by a WHS (UK) or Marshaltown (USA) trowel, quite another to tell people there is only one way to use it. It may be that due to a glitch in archaeological history, an isolated group of Britons are using the terms "context recording/Harris matrix" as a nickname for stratigraphic excavation, something that has, of course, been around very much longer and is a great deal more versatile. But even stratigraphic excavation is not the only way of making history from archaeology, as we shall see in Chapter 2.

Wheeler's second sure prediction, the end of the test pit, has not come about at all, even in England. The test pit is now probably the most common method of excavation worldwide, and dominates archaeology in America. Furthermore, the pits are mostly dug by *schnitt* or, as it is variously termed, "arbitrary level" or "unit level." One reason for this is that strata are often hard to see. Another is that it has become a standard default practice. The most widely used US manual in its 7th edition tells us: "The unit-level method is undoubtedly the most common method of excavating sites that show little stratigraphic variation" (Hester et al. 1997, 88). While the doyen of US cultural resource management (CRM) insists that archaeology is a toolbox, and there is no standard way of carrying out fieldwork (King 2005, 50–52), other textbooks acknowledge a different reality: "The one-meter square is still the first thing that most beginning archaeologists in this country [USA] learn to recognize as the basic excavation unit. Square-hole archaeology is a tradition and very widespread default method in American archaeology." Furthermore, "default methods are particularly rampant in all aspects of CRM work" (Black and Jolly 2003, 16).

## THEORY, IN PRACTICE

Whether the test pit arrived out of convenience or caution or thrift, it was soon sanctified by theory. Anthropologists of the 1960s, famously Lewis Binford, regarded the archaeological deposit as a fossilized social system, and like a modern community, the scientific way to interrogate such a system was via sampling (Binford 1964; 1972). The main instrument used by social scientists is the sample questionnaire—get enough of them filled in, review the collected data statistically—and bingo!—you have discovered a behavioral trend ("a significant number of vegetarians go jogging").

In archaeological fieldwork, the equivalent of the questionnaire was the square-meter sample, randomly placed, either applied to material lying on the surface or for strata in the shape of an excavated test pit. This was used both to explore a buried community as a research project, and to check out a piece of land that was to be disturbed, where a 15% random sample was deemed representative of the whole occupation. This scientific, or social scientific, approach was known colloquially as the "new archaeology" or as "processual archaeology," since its objectives included understanding the systems that governed human communities and the processes that caused them to change.

Binford knew that the key to the execution of fieldwork was design (1964). While Wheeler had set the tone by his advocacy of "having a plan" (1956, 239), Binford wanted the plan to demonstrate itself worthy of the objective: a plan that stated which data were to be recovered and subjected to which analysis, with which end in view. He was sure that he was doing science, and his many admirers have remained sure of it since. Here is Patty Jo Watson, restaking the claim in 2007: "The core of Americanist archaeology today is still New Archaeology, revised and modified by practitioners and critics to take its place within archaeological thought around the world" (in her foreword to Skibo et al. 2007).

For all their differences in the field, the "single contexters" and the "new archaeologists" continue to yearn for an integrated, unified discipline with common goals and methods worldwide. They want to be like geology, like chemistry. They want to recover data and store it up. They want the results of fieldwork to mean the same wherever they are, in whichever period. Keith Kintigh's comments in 2006 are typical: "It is imperative that the development of a cyberinfrastructure for archaeology begin immediately," he says; "there is a pressing need for an archaeological information infrastructure that will allow us to archive, access, integrate and mine disparate data sets" (Kintigh 2006, 577). And here is Binford himself in 2007: "The past . . . is not a sick patient in need of diagnosis: it is a segment of a diverse and highly variable structured system variously preserved in the present." He takes issue with Brian Fagan who had somewhat eccentrically wanted universities to focus their syllabi on CRM in the present day, rather than on the rediscovery of the past. Binford says: "Giving up scientific goals for legislated goals with no practical developmental research strategies carried from one project to another is not the path of the future archaeology. A better response to Fagan would be that we do not need to reduce academic training but we should instead abandon the non-productive eclectic humanistic approach to the education of all archaeologists" (2007, 240).

The eclectic humanistic elephant-in-the-room that Binford is trying to heave out is identifiable as processualism's would-be successor, postmodernist archaeology as promoted by Ian Hodder in Cambridge and now developed from his new base at Stanford University in California (e.g., 1997; 1999; 2005). Just as processual archaeology developed from anthropology's search for explanations for social change, so archaeology took its next inspiration from anthropology's development of structural, symbolic, and reflexive ideas. When an indigenous person was asked a question by an anthropologist, the answer might well be mischievous, invented, or what they thought you wanted to hear. In any case, it wasn't data. After Lévi Strauss, this prompted closer attention to critique. After Jacques Derrida, the agenda swung to the deconstruction of the interlocutor: Why did they say what they said? What was the motive behind the untruth? This mapped onto archaeological ideas of agency and structuration, the discovery of the motivation behind tombs, buildings, and monuments. The path followed by "post-processualists" led easily enough into current anthropological anxieties about the colonial nature of scientific characterization itself; even where they were apparently irrational, the versions of the past professed by traditional peoples demanded respect to the same degree as their own territories and customs. "Multivocality" is the replacement of a single synthesis or model with multiple strands of interpretation. "Reflexivity" is the recognition that, just as we discover motivations behind the narratives of others, so we need to be aware of similar tendencies toward preferred styles of tale-telling in ourselves (references and summaries in Carver 2002, 469–470).

This approach has much potential to influence modern fieldwork. Ian Hodder certainly thinks so and has offered us a case study in Çatalhöyük and a treatise in his *Archaeological Process* (2005; 1999). The main exhortation, to bring interpretation back on site, is encapsulated in his attractive phrase "at the trowel's edge" (cf. 1997). However, the impact of the post-processual stance in fieldwork has been very uneven, perhaps partly due to factors about to be

24

explored here. Some aspects of Hodder's program, such as recording the recording, were already widely practiced, though probably not widely appreciated; other desirables, like a permanent specialist presence on site, were often intended, but dependent on a high level of funding. But other aspects, like the lack of a published project design, need to be challenged—and they will be. However, on a visit to Çatalhöyük itself, one is gladdened to find a very well-founded, well-managed research excavation, expertly supervised by Shahina Farid. That is to say, in spite of all the multivocal and reflexive claims that have been made, the excavation methodology is conventional and hierarchical, with a linear design.

The age-old ding-dong about whether archaeology is an art or a science has been largely captured by academics who have made it into a debate about theory and, in particular, about the nature of reasoning and interpretation. This is a pity. All subjects wrestle with this kind of self-definition, so obviously we will too; but it doesn't make us special. What makes us special is what we do; and what we do, that no-one else does, is field archaeology. My mission in these chapters is to install field archaeology—archaeological investigation—as the central axis of our subject. What students do in the field is not a recreation for university vacations; it is the basis of the syllabus and the source of virtually all the jobs. We should take it seriously. My way of doing this is to elevate the whole practice as something creative and original and life-enhancing. We are not analyzing the past or reading it; we are writing it, and we do this through design.

Processual and post-processual procedures are different aspects of the same inquiry. A living community can be interrogated either by asking its members to fill up census forms or by spending long evenings talking in the pub; the information gathered relates to different kinds of equally valid generality. If such analogies have any merit, we will need to create a field archaeology that can serve either approach—the data-driven and the discourse-driven—and to make it work within the confines of a single opportunity. This task will be addressed in a little while (see Chapter 5, p. 132). Now it is necessary to set out the menu for the book as a whole and say where it and I are coming from.

## CONFESSIONS OF A FREE-LANCE

In his enduring synthesis, *Ancient Europe* (1965), Stuart Piggott discussed the matters of what would become "archaeological theory" with exhilarating prescience. Anticipating the "reflexive" stance, he commented: "We interpret the evidence in terms of our own intellectual make-up, conditioned as it is by the period and culture with which we were brought up, our social and religious background, our current assumptions and presuppositions and our age and status." He continues: "Few have faced this with the honesty of Mr. Osbert Lancaster, who prefaced a book with the words 'My criteria, political, architectural and scenic, remain firmly Anglo-Saxon, and the standards of judgment are also those of an Anglican graduate of Oxford with a taste for architecture, turned cartoonist, approaching middle age and living in Kensington'. Similar acts of self-revelation," says Piggott, "would contribute greatly to our understanding of historical scholarship" (Piggott 1965, 5). While not really aspiring to too much in the way of historical scholarship, I nevertheless ask that the self-indulgent comments that follow be accepted in such a spirit of explanatory confession.

When I came to field archaeology, ex army, in 1971, there were three main emphases in active theory: anthropological, historical, and empirical; there were three main kinds of excavation layout: pit, box, and area; and there were three main ways of dissecting a deposit: slicing through it, exposing it in area, or lifting it in predefined contexts. We were taught that these had replaced each other in some kind evolutionary sequence. I was soon to find out that this was a highly Anglo-centric view of the world, since all were still active and still being promoted somewhere with equal passion. I should explain that (like Piggott) I do not have a degree in archaeology, so my credentials are fairly suspect. I was educated at military colleges, at Sandhurst when I was 17, and Shrivenham when I was in my late 20s. At Sandhurst I learned SMEAC, the mantra of the troop leader required to manage a battle (see Chapter 5, p. 132). You had to have a plan—this is where Wheeler got it from, of course—and the plan had parts to it, each worked out in great detail. The Duke of Wellington famously said: "No plan survives the first hour of battle." So why have one? Why have a precise, logical, controlled procedure for an activity that actually depends on a thousand chance encounters and individual responses? But as Wellington knew, to surrender oneself to chance is pre-emptively to invite defeat. His views on battle were powered by ideas that archaeological excavators will recognize: "All the business of war, and indeed all the business of life, is to endeavour to find out what you don't know, by what you do" (Knowles 1999, 809).

My academic education at Shrivenham was in maths—which gave me a tendency to put everything into sets; and in chemistry, a discipline that required you to declare your aims and methods, and record carefully in the lab the changing signals of something you never got to see. These are hard things to lose even if you become a writer or a historian, and they are stratified into my version of archaeological investigation. My first encounter with this arcane business was in 1971 at Winchester, a town that lies within mo-ped distance of Selbourne where we then lived. Having spent a week mending windows of the old school at Lower Brooke Street, I was invited with a handful of other volunteers to work with Martin Biddle at the Roman South Gate, which survived as a large, impenetrable pair of mortared flint piers refurbished in the 9th century by King Alfred. I found Biddle a most inspiring companion, troweling, searching, chatting away about the layers as we tried to define them, referring to them—as was the fashion of those days—by nicknames, often associated with food—the sickly grit, the nutty crunch, the Dundee cake, and so on. These were later recorded in more sober language and drawn with precision, but what I want to remember now, in the light of later theorizing and moralizing, is the equable and affable nature of the almost continuous sharing of ideas —and this from a very senior operator, often criticized in my hearing for his commanding attitude.

Also in mo-ped range in 1971 was the excavation of an Anglo-Saxon village at Chalton, revealed when Peter Addyman and David Leigh stripped the thin topsoil from the surface of the chalk. In comparison to Winchester, this was children's archaeology. We brushed the chalk carefully until little gray spots appeared on the surface and then sprinkled it with water; at this point the spots went black and turned into a post-hole building which could be clearly seen and photographed from the top of a tower. I wasn't a bit surprised to note that our methods and records were quite different from those of Winchester. Of course, it was a different kind of site, both now and in the past. I would no more have expected the same plan of attack for a farmhouse in Picardy and a swamp in Malaya.

Peter took me to York with him and gave me my first break—the supervision of the excavation of a car park at St Mary Bishophill, where I became a feral digger and grew lots of hair. In accordance with the Barkerian ethos of the day, the site was to be excavated layer by layer, every part earning equal attention, but confining ourselves to the deposit that was to be destroyed by developers. We encountered a 19th-century theodolite factory, superseding an 18th-century mansion (Fairfax House), dug into a mass of medieval pits that chopped up the floors and foundations of a robbed-out Roman town house. It was plain that the dissection of this mass of disturbed layers one at a time would take years rather than the months we had.

This was 1973, and the "context card" had just been introduced, a one-page questionnaire designed to record every stratigraphic unit in a standardized manner. The scientific character of the new format gave these records primacy over the old site journal, which we were enjoined to jettison. So we filled in the cards, but I always found it impossible to dig without interpreting—that is, wondering what I was looking at. I enjoyed playing *I-spy* and *Botticelli* like everyone else, but just troweling and periodically interrupting the game to fill up a context card was not my idea of digging: it didn't amount to an *investigation*. Duty done to the new standardized recording system, I would sit for hours with my A4 black book, making sketches and diagrams and dreaming about what it might all mean.

This turned out to be useful. For reasons never adequately explained, the plans and context records relating to Bishophill Senior disappeared in the archives of the York Archaeological Trust, and the site had to be written up largely from my "black book," plus a typescript I made before departing (Carver et al. 1978). That doesn't make proforma recording wrong, but it did convince me that abandoning the site journal (the recording of the recording, and the recording of the changing interpretation) was premature. I also felt that we would have spent our time and money better if we had known what to expect in advance, and cut our cloth according to what we wanted to know and the means we had available.

This was the first stirring of what was to become "evaluation," and I went on to develop it over the next few years at Durham and in the West Midlands and in Italy and France. I knew that Martin Biddle had introduced a similar kind of selectivity at Winchester, but that was in a research project, in which the undug places were not going to be destroyed. At Saddler Street in Durham I tested all four areas available—settling on an area under the basement of the old theater, where the ground smelled like wet blankets and proved indeed to contain wonderfully preserved wood. Faced with posts with the birch bark still on, with midden heaps containing old shoes and wattle buildings, I recognized that simply to turn strata into contexts was a quite inadequate way of recording them—necessary, but not sufficient. It seemed to me that while every stratigraphic unit should be recorded as a context, there were sets of contexts that had a more advanced meaning; a storage pit, for example, was a set of its cut, its lining, and whatever was in it. This set, this higher-level entity, was termed a "feature"; I also decided that there were sets of features that belonged together, like the post-hole buildings at Chalton; this even higher-level entity earned the designation of "structure." An archaeological deposit could therefore be resolved into contexts, some sets of which could be resolved into features, which in turn could sometimes be resolved into structures. Each was a set of the others. I then put these different entities into a diagram that showed the sequence. This diagram later became such a provocative issue with champions of the Harris matrix—not least Ed himself, whom I wasn't to meet until the following year—that I shall have to revisit it. I hope to convince you that when all is said and done, these are just diagrams, not magic spells, only useful insofar as they achieve what they intend (Chapter 2).

Meanwhile, in the West Midlands, I continued to learn that town sites are different from one another, even in the same town. And I went on learning the same lesson in work done for the French and Italian governments. I noted that there was a relationship between the topography of a site, the base material on which it stood, and the strata that formed and survived. When an excavation happened, I saw that the *research dividend*, as we started to call it, could be maximized with the use of "recovery levels"—different degrees of digging and recording to match different tasks (p. 125). Therefore, the information we retrieved from an archaeological site was really a function of how hard we looked—just as Petrie had implied.

I had plenty of opportunities to point this out to Phil Barker, who was emerging as the excavator's guru in the 1970s, since I shared an office with him in Worcester. He maintained, with unfailing courtesy, that I was mistaken. If you looked from the top at a perfectly clean surface, everyone would see the same thing. If every excavator were to see something different, our subject would not exist. The prescription was perfectly clean surfaces. I agreed with this, but reminded him how Hope-Taylor had seen different lines on the surface of the gravel at Yeavering (see Chapter 4), depending on how long ago it had stopped raining: there's an optimum image and it is determined by us, by how carefully we had cleaned, how long we waited, how hard we looked. Barker was right that immaculate cleaning is essential. But that is not all you do. There is an evaluation stage, which tells us how the archaeology survives in the ground, and a strategy stage which tells us what we have to do to see it. Since what we see depends on how hard we look, an archaeological investigation is not only determined by its objectives, but by its terrain.

In the further interests of self-revelation, I have three more significant memories to offer from the particularity of my own experience. In the 1970s, perhaps in nostalgia for my army days, I became convinced that there was a staged sequence for fieldwork, the thing I now called "field research procedure" or FRP (Chapter 5). The stages had different purposes, and each one led to the next, like the plan and execution and reporting of a battle. By the time I was asked to do Sutton Hoo in 1982, this seemed to me a good way to do research projects too, and I asked my employers, the Sutton Hoo Research Trust, for three years to put together a fully costed project design, which they agreed to. This design would match the *terrain* (that is, the archaeology surviving in this pillaged cemetery dug into acid sand) with our *objectives* (to discover the social and ideological changes experienced in early England).

But I soon realized that this version of project design of the early 1980s, like Binford's in the 1960s and 1970s, lacked an essential component which was coming to the fore particularly in Australia and America: the social context in which our work was to take place. This was something else that Petrie knew about. He said: "In archaeology there is perhaps a greater range of ethical questions, of the individual versus the community, than in any other science" (1904, 169). At Sutton Hoo we had a wide range of stakeholders (as it became fashionable to call them): landowners, the government, academic historians, and, most influentially, local people who took their dogs for a walk on the mounds. There was also the cohort of the unborn, those to whom we owed something of this monument's survival, as well as its story. Of all who submitted research designs for Sutton Hoo, I was the only one who drew back from "total excavation"—which thus came very close to happening. My idea for "targeted" excavation ran counter to the current of the day, which said that only the excavation of the whole site would tell us the answer, whatever the question. My position was that the question determined the answer, and if the question demanded the excavation of the whole site, it was the wrong question and we should think again. I had similar reservations about the random sampling that was becoming popular in parts of the academy. To choose mounds at random would be obtuse, the chances of understanding the spaces in between with test pits were slim, and their likely impact would be the reduction of visibility in the long term. I adopted the concept of the *ethical stance*, things we would not do because they were unethical, because they deprived the unborn of their birthright. The design thus confined itself to the part we could justify and knew how to dig. The rest of the site, 75% of it as so far known, would wait for the future (Carver 2005, chap. 2).

A few years later, at Achir south of the Atlas Mountains in Algeria, I encountered another kind of ethical restraint (FIG. 1.3). Once we had defined the 10th-century Fatimid town at Benia, the Algerian government wanted us

FIGURE 1.3. Benia low town, part of the Achir group of 10th- to 12th-century settlements on the Haut Plateau between the Atlas Mountains and the Sahara Desert, Algeria. Researchers and officials stand on the sweep of the buried town wall. The interior of the early Islamic town, now cultivated, lies to the right (*photo by the author*).

to clear farmers from inside the enclosure, ban plowing, and make it into a monument. This seemed rash: it would have alienated every farmer on the Haut Plateau for no reason: what was plowed was plowed, and might as well go on being plowed by local persons, who also had every reason to take care of the site and see off intruders. The ground was very dusty and needed water to improve definition; and water was in short supply. The research objective (mainly to make a comparative study of Roman and Islamic agriculture) was intriguing but sensitive: our project team contained Francophile, Francophobe, agnostic, devout Islamic, and fundamentalist Islamic participants, generating dialogues of impenetrable density, and resulting in my eventual public denunciation as a spy in 1993. At this point, my role in the project was prudently terminated. The evaluation seasons had been a success, and the historical sequence and tourist potential were well profiled (Carver and Soudi 1996). But the time was not right for an investigation into the role of early Islam in enlarging the economy of the southern Mediterranean. Each of the participants had a special mission for the past, and the idea of design, which I promoted, required compromise and consensus. This was not to be.

A more recent project at Portmahomack in Easter Ross, Scotland, involved excavation on a smooth, silty damp sand, a joy to trowel. Sprayed with water and looked at from a tower, it offered a marvelously detailed definition (FIG. 1.4). The research objectives were not controversial: we were looking for a settlement of the Picts at the time that their kingdom formed. But the social context was no less complex than Algeria. Northeast Scotland has some 42 recorded varieties of Christianity, and their adherents all seemed to have a view on what should happen to the redundant church of St Colman, and indeed how the monastery beneath it had come about. We had many different sources of funding and many partners in the venture. Some local people wanted tourism, others didn't; some liked history, others regarded it as a personal affront; some locals just didn't like other locals. Some regarded the conversion of the building into a piece of heritage to be an ideological conversion as nearly as fundamental as those from the Catholic to the Presbyterian and then to the Free Church. We found that "local" was by no means the homogeneous descendant community we assumed it to be; it was riven by class, adopted ethnicity,

FIGURE 1.4. Strip-and-map area excavation in operation at Portmahomack, northeast Scotland, using students in a troweling line, a tower, and a surface sprayed with water (*photo by the author*).

and vested interests. But eventually all of these were united by the desire for funding, and aligned with one of three main players: the Tarbat Trust, which aimed for the restoration of a beloved landmark; the Highland Council, which wanted a museum and center of education for its area of jurisdiction; and the University of York, whose aim was to discover the origin and fate of the Christian Pictish kingdom. The amount of earth that needed to be moved to answer this question was great—at least a hectare of excavation—as was the money consequently needed to pay professional archaeologists. The project was too big to be funded by a national research council, but risked making no sense if it were smaller. By creating a common objective in the restoration of the church and the creation of a museum within it, furnished by the findings of the research, the project could attract funding (in the millions) from the Heritage Lottery fund. Thus, the design of the project did not require us to run up a flag to a particular theory or impose a standardized methodology; the task was to reconcile the archaeological objectives to the terrain and the social, economic, and political circumstances in which we found ourselves (Carver 2008).

## THE PATH OF DESIGN

It is very likely that other archaeologists have navigated between their ambitions and the realities of life in a similar way and are, no doubt, equally prone to making a virtue of their compromises. Looking back now, I am sure that flexibility and opportunism are intrinsic talents of our particular metier. Like Wheeler, I believe that there is no one right way of doing archaeology, but, unlike Wheeler, I mean it. There is an infinite number of right ways, provided you justify them by design: doing field archaeology is not a matter of being right or wrong, but of being appropriate. What is done in the field cannot proceed from a theory and must not rely on a single method. This is not because archaeology is an art rather than a science, but because it is an art and a science and a social science. It is a historical pursuit deploying scientific procedures in a social arena. The way this is achieved, as it is in architecture, sculpture, novel writing, building a motorway, or going to the moon, is by design. There is no trick here and no dogma. Design is different for every project, and all method and theory are subsumed in the design process.

Archaeological design, like architectural design, is harnessed creativity, creativity with an inspired but practical outcome. The public can be protected from bad architecture by the application of industrial standards. Archaeology too requires standards of investigation and recording; but these are part of the equipment, necessary but not sufficient. Standards are one thing, standardization another—the first essential, the second, inhibiting. Every archaeological project requires a design in which objectives, methods, recovery levels, and conservation needs are all spelled out. In CRM mitigation projects, the use of so-called boilerplate, where one description of work procedures is simply pasted onto the next project proposal, is accepting the dogma of the standardized response, accepting that every excavation should be done in exactly the same way. This ignores the inherent variability of all the salient factors: the objectives, the terrain, the social context. A high standard and the use of a clear descriptive vocabulary are both essential to fieldwork; that is an unassailable principle. Quite different is the standardization of the whole response: the use of the same tools, the same program of investigation, the same recording package, the same descriptors, on every occasion in every country. By recording all excavations in the same way, we lose more through a lack of sensitivity than we gain from adhering to a discipline. We would not ask our architects, our artists, our journalists, to build, paint, and write in an identical style.

In my way of thinking, what you do in the field depends on the research agenda, the terrain, and the social context in which you work: what you want to know, what you can know, and what you are permitted to investigate, at any particular place and time (cf. Carman 2004). These things must be discovered during a preliminary stage, the evaluation stage, and then matched to one another in the form of a design. Art and science, a curiosity about people, and an analytical method of inquiry are all necessary for our mission; so they are necessary too for our successful execution of the mission. In this we align wholly with neither chemistry nor human intuition, but make use of both, like medicine (Carver 2002, 489). Our objectives will include the big picture: the community and its culture, what happened to them, and why and what made them change; and the intimate picture: how these people perceived one another, the landscape, their past. Clearly these objectives will not surrender to a single technique.

Our raw materials are amazingly varied: the stuff we work on can be rock, marsh, or field, and we can encounter strata on top of a mountain or under the sea—a big wide world of different terrain. This geographic and geological circumstance provides field archaeology's arena: whatever we want to know, the terrain is determinant of what we can see and the means we will need to see it. As I show in Chapter 2, we have greatly enlarged what we expect from excavation, from the definition of a layer and its interface, to variations in the smallest grains of minerals, and into the molecules within. It no longer fits into the specifications still accepted as adequate by the commercial or the research sectors.

Our work takes place out-of-doors on land, in public and for the public; it is deeply embedded in society. People care about what we find—for ill or good. Some are reluctant to have their time on earth interrupted with bad news from the country of the dead: the past is an irrelevance and an impedance, and archaeologists are a pain. Others feel that the land of the dead is *their* land and lay claim to it. Doing good fieldwork requires money. Who is to do it, who is to pay, and why? All these matters, also determinant for what is done, arise from the social context of the fieldworker. In our crew, in our locality, in our country, and on our continent, we are in a social, political, and economic situation that controls what field archaeologists can do.

This applies also to those who confront archaeology's version of the past and believe that the vision of their tradition or their faith is equally valid. Part of the success of the postmodern platform comes from the realization that just as science challenged religion in the 19th century, so religion is challenging science in the late 20th. An estimated 80% of the world's population subscribes to faiths that the remaining 20% would regard as irrational, and these latter naturally prefer to rationalize the rights of the irrational rather than fight them. One sensible response is to accept that religion does not have a monopoly on ethics. If this is so, we don't need to soften our deductive desires to avoid giving offense—we need to harden our ethical framework as it applies to archaeology, to protect the interests of our fellows: to make new knowledge while doing no harm. Here I am going to take ethics as the foundation of archaeology's social context—the subject of Chapter 3.

Objective, terrain, social context—what we want to know, out of what remains, out of what we can access: this is what makes field archaeology happen and explains why it is different every time and everywhere. The result of undertaking a short tour of the world (Chapter 4) is to emphasize the variety of terrain and social context and, in consequence, the designs that people come up with: flexibility of mind finds diversity on the ground. Those who don't want it to be this varied urge us to go for the box, the random test pit, the stratigraphic context, procedures in which we feel safe. But my mission is to persuade you that those days are gone. Research agenda, terrain, and social context must be assessed every time by evaluation, and reconciled through design, and implemented with the largest possible toolbox, in which nothing is forbidden. My hope is that this will be seen not as anarchy, but strength.

# CHAPTER 2

# MEGA, MACRO, MICRO, NANO:
# DIALOGUES WITH TERRAIN

## INTRODUCTION

Meeting a fellow human for the first time, we observe his or her clothes, the outer form, the face, the voice—aspects that make up a personality. A doctor can probe under the skin, to the flesh, the bones, the molecules, to diagnose some biological trends for good or ill in among the complexities of the flesh. In a person, there are thus certain properties, like the face, that are unique, hard to deconstruct precisely and yet unmistakable to another human. There are others, like the length of a femur or a blood-group, that can be scientifically classified. An archaeological site also has a layered personality: superficial aspects that are striking and hard to categorize, and underneath, deposits of diverse materials, variously interleaved, and of different sizes. Like a human body, the characteristics are best appreciated in a multi-conceptual manner: at one level we use our scientific tool kit, at another our human intuition.

Archaeological investigation aims to write the history of sites and landscapes with a view to enlarging, enriching, and understanding better what humans did there. In my contention, our ability to do this depends on successfully matching what we want to know with what is left on, and under, the ground. But when considering the question of what's left, the subject of this chapter, we have to appreciate that archaeological monuments, sites, and strata do not lie supine awaiting rediscovery; what we see depends on the measures we take to see it; what we see is what we seek. Thus our question about the big underground is not so much "what is there?" but "what can be defined by us today, and how?"

The underground world is startlingly different everywhere we go: buried under dunes, in caves, in swamps, underwater, on chalk, on clay, in tells, in steaming jungles, and frozen under permafrost. It is also startlingly complex; reaching down and grabbing a handful of garden soil, Richard Dawkins announced that there were four times as many microorganisms in his handful than there were people on earth. "Soil" is only one type of archaeological deposit and not the most important for us: we know what it was for (i.e., to grow crops), and although there are few things more satisfying for gardeners and farmers, not even they would claim that all human life is to be found there. For this reason, as we'll see, the methods of soil science won't map onto the needs of archaeology.

What we need to define varies in scale from the very big to the very small —from the monument to the microbe, the *mega* to the *nano*, and our ability to identify these is accelerating. Sixty years ago archaeologists began routinely to collect the bones of animals as well as humans; fifty years ago Stuart Streuver was extracting plant remains at the Koster site by flotation (Streuver 1968); forty years ago Sebastian Payne was urging excavators to use sieves to find smaller mammals, birds, and fish (Payne 1972); thirty years ago Harry Kenward was showing what could be done with insects (Kenward 1978). Twenty years ago Richard Evershed was extracting lipids from the walls of pots and the innards of Lindow man (Evershed and Connolly 1988; Evershed et al. 1991); ten years ago we were learning how to interpret isotope signatures trapped in teeth (Stuart-Williams et al. 1996) and isolating DNA in bones (Brown 2001); two years ago we were identifying it in the soil (Hebsgaard et al. 2009); and last year the proteins extracted from bone fragments led to the recognition of animal species (Buckley et al. 2009). TABLE 2.1 sums it up.

Note that, in archaeology, nothing stops being interesting, so the shopping list gets potentially longer at every site. I say potentially, because although the tool kit is bigger, not everything can be applied everywhere. It all depends on the terrain. In addition, the appropriate tools are often not applied for quite different reasons—such as a reluctance to spend money. To this we will return. Meanwhile, reviewing the current operation from larger to smaller gives us as convenient a way as any to structure our agenda.

## MEGA

In most countries, the archaeological units of interest are the landscape, the site, and the building, each of which has an academic as well as a social mean-

Table 2.1. Targets: The onward march of excavator ambition

| | MEGA | MACRO | MICRO | NANO |
|---|---|---|---|---|
| *Recovery method/yield* | *Pick and shovel* | *Trowel, brush, and screen* | *Sampling* | *Subsampling* |
| 1800 | Pots Statues | | | |
| 1850 | " | Jewelry Sherds Coins | | |
| 1900 | " | Animals | | |
| 1950 | " | Plants | Fish Birds | |
| 1960 | " | " | Seeds Pollen | |
| 1980 | " | " | Insects Phytoliths | |
| 1990 | " | " | " | Lipids |
| 2000 | " | " | " | Isotope signatures |
| 2005 | " | " | " | aDNA |
| 2010 | " | " | " | Proteins |

ing. In practice, these represent packages of potential information, and we are led to them through survey, chance, or hunch. While a castle is fairly easy to recognize, other kinds of sites and landscapes are more exotic, and we may not be able to guess where the edges are or give them a name. The frequency and density of ancient material encountered in the ground in Europe have encouraged the use of the new term "historic environment." This can mean all surviving cultural material, as a parallel to the natural environment, and is no doubt intended to attract a similar following. In the journal of the same name, the remit of historic environment has been extended to include anything cultural that has ever happened or still is happening (King 2010). This is a heady concept, and I shall confine myself to more familiar targets.

Historic landscapes, sites, and buildings are being continually defined on the basis of their surface appearance, their "face." We live among them, exploit them, extoll them, enhance them, imitate them, maim them, restore them, and destroy them; and this "management" of cultural resources is how the majority of archaeologists earn their living. The large-scale patterns produced by the distribution of historic sites represent both the modern repertoire of cultural property and, more obscurely, the ancient geography of settlement. The status of such patterns, drawn from detailed surveys on the ground and in the air, naturally occasions much debate. Do they amount to ancient landscapes which require conservation, like random holes in a moth-eaten blanket? Or are they predominantly landscapes of the imagination, as evocative as poetry but harder to keep from under a motorway?

In methods of investigation, landscape archaeology is moving away from random sampling and toward tiered evaluation, where each level of survey leads to another that is more intense (Carver 2009, 82); and to multi-conceptual definitions that rise from the factual ("pottery scatters") to the interpretive ("industrial settlement"). Investigating a landscape thus becomes more like investigating a large, shallow site, and in research the same imperatives apply: to match the objectives to the terrain and to the social contexts of ownership, use, and local expectation.

The study of *terrain* at the scale of a landscape is worthy of urgent research and development. The way sites show from the air is thought to depend on a number of factors, such as crop, contour, and moisture deficit; but it has not yet reached the stage of being readily predictable. From a satellite, definition depends on the type of sensors employed, visual or thermal. For any aerial platform, success appears to improve with multi-sensor capability: not just using photographs to record contrasting reflections of light of various wavelengths, but lidar (light detection and ranging) to report small undulations in the surface, and radar to report buried horizons such as bands of peat. Lidar, which fires a laser range-finder at the ground from an airplane, can resolve the response into two signals—first pulse (FP) and last pulse (LP). Over woodland, the first pulse corresponds to the tree canopy and the last to the ground beneath, thus mapping earthworks concealed from sight—as in Bernard Devereux's lidar survey of Welshbury hillfort, which achieved the same resolution beneath the trees as the rig and furrow viewed in open country in the neighborhood (Devereux et al. 2005). On wetland, FP/LP seems to relate to the current ground surface and the surface of the rock head, so that it effectively measures the thickness of peat or alluvium. In Andy Howard's Trent Valley survey, he found he was getting a number of responses from different depths, equivalent to different horizons of peat layers (Howard et al. 2008). He checked these thicknesses with GPR (ground penetrating radar; Conyers 2010) and dated the layers with OSL (optically stimulated luminescence; Grün 2001) and radiocarbon dating. The result was something resembling a chronological map of wetland landscape (see also Challis et al. 2008).

On the ground, we are getting new levels of precision from Total Station topographical survey, and from geophysics, georadar, and chemical mapping (Faßbinder and Irlinger 1996; Gaffney 2008; Jordan 2009; Becker 2008 [caesium]; GPR: Leckebusch 2003; Trinks et al. 2008; 2009). At Shapwick, the landscape of a village was explored (among other ways) by mapping metal salts in the topsoil, a measure that led to the detection of an abandoned medieval churchyard through the concentration of lead from its coffins (Aston et al. 1998). This project was also notable for its inclusion of large numbers of volunteers, something that contributed to the intensity of the results as much as the science—a theme to which we will return. Another landscape mapping method that is proving useful in England is the portable antiquities scheme, whereby metal objects found by treasure hunters with metal detectors are declared and recorded (Bland 2005). This has resulted in a veritable flood of recorded discoveries (66,311 in 2007). However, the purpose of the exercise is not merely to make distribution maps, but to use them for research. In a project focused on Norfolk, Mary Chester-Kaldwell mapped the harvest of Anglo-Saxon objects recovered by treasure hunters, but then qualified the pattern by examining the way the data had been found. She noted that metal-detectorist search strategies are gregarious—they tend to follow previous sightings, like bird watchers; but their success when they get to a fruitful area has been shown to depend on terrain, depth, and the machine employed. The distribution of material is thus representative of the Anglo-Saxons, but mediated and qualified by the behavior of metal-detectorists. In the emerging pattern, cemeteries could be distinguished from settlements using the type of object that tends to turn up in each, and in consequence the settlements could be assigned to the cemetery they used—information that has eluded every other type of research (Chester-Kaldwell 2008).

It is not impossible that even our most careful investigations are failing to see a whole type of site, one that survives only as a ghost in the plow soil. Immo Trinks (pers. comm.; and see Trinks et al. 2008; 2009) has been collecting examples of these ghost sites and divides them into three kinds. In the first, the anomaly is detected by aerial reconnaissance or geophysics, but only exists in the topsoil where it remains as a kind of "dark soil sausage." This seems to have been the case with a georadar survey conducted in December 2008 near the medieval monastery of St. Olof in Skänninge, Sweden. In a second type, also from Sweden, prehistoric ditches that never cut the subsoil nevertheless left their drainage pattern there—subsequently picked up by geophysical survey sensitive to differences in water content. In a third example, a set of row-graves in Bavaria was seen in an air photograph. Subsequent magnetic survey did not detect the row graves, but did find ring ditches with central graves. But excavation to subsoil found neither. By chance the site was subsequently left open, and the ring ditches, but no graves, appeared after two weeks, simply by weathering.

These comments serve to indicate that the concept of "landscape survey" is evolving from a fresh-air stroll by the explorer (although this has lost none of its value) to a multi-tool inquiry, in which the diverse properties of the surface, or near-surface, may be mapped in different ways. Plainly this kind of layered inquiry, with its consequent layers of meaning, will require a carefully designed and staged approach, going well beyond the superficial inventory of surface indications that is often held to suffice for management purposes. This problem will need revisiting in Chapter 5. For now, let's narrow the focus to a patch of ground made attractive by survey and subject it to closer scrutiny. If the value of archaeological investigation lies in its story, our approach to terrain should be the definition of the entities through which that story may be told.

## MACRO

There is an immediate difference in character as between a well-stratified and an unstratified deposit, which in turn prompts a difference in approach and, in fact, a whole difference in philosophy. In very general terms, well-stratified sites prompt a macro-response—that is, a response to the stratigraphic interfaces that are evident. However, where strata are invisible or hard to define, obstinate excavators have been driven to make more of them, and the result has been progress in micro- and nano-definition, something we will pursue below. In practice, most sites are neither fully stratified nor hopelessly unstratified, so there will be considerable crossovers between them. Excavators need to be as versatile as their sites are varied, and what I would like to urge is that we enlarge the toolbox, put more options in the hands of project designers, and cast a little doubt on the wisdom of applying standard procedures, invariably, whether in town or country.

Three decades of site formation studies have shown us that an archaeological site is not a static system, but a dynamic one, in which artifacts, bones, and seeds are potentially on the move (Schiffer 1987; Tryon 2006). We therefore *define* rather than record what we see. Macro distinctions—that is, those visible to the naked eye—depend on deposits of different colors and textures and the interfaces between them. If you look at a section, these distinctions can be seen, and defined—that is, recorded as entities. This process turns a pile of earth and stones into structures, activities, episodes, and events (FIG. 2.1). However, in looking at a section, or a surface (cf. FIG. 1.4), different people will see different numbers of interfaces, depending on what they know how to recognize. Furthermore, the number you see depends on how hard you look; if you clean very carefully and enhance with a light spray, you will see more layers than if you tidied up the surface with a shovel. One way of monitoring this is by using the recovery levels, a process that does at least determine in a well-ordered way the tools to be used and the records to be made (see Chapter 5, p. 125).

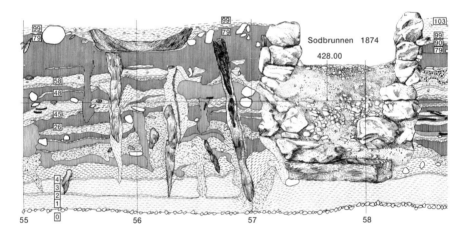

FIGURE 2.1. A drawn section through part of the Neolithic lake village at Twann, Canton Bern, Switzerland. The lake bed is at the bottom, and a Bronze Age dugout boat (shown in cross section), *top left*, with a stone-lined well dug in 1874 (*top right*). The drawing depicts the strata using conventions for clay and silt, with the organic occupation sediments numbered. The granule-size and degree of mixing is recorded separately for each deposit, and conserved in a sample. Rather than a record of decisions made on site about the order of deposition, this type of drawing attempts to capture details of formation processes and the stratigraphic position of posts allowing for later reinterpretation. The section was captured in the north face of a trench 160 m long, 14.5 m wide, and more than 2 m deep dug in advance of motorway construction (Ammann et al. 1977, fig. 2, showing profile X in section 8. Scale in meters; *courtesy of the Archaeology Service, Canton of Bern*).

In corollary, how hard you look predetermines how carefully you record. There is no sense in sieving a pit full of bricks, or surveying to the nearest millimeter a ditch unearthed by a bulldozer. Later we will see how recovery levels also serve the design of projects, in deciding what must be done and what it will need to cost. For the moment, let's just agree that a context needs a recovery level; otherwise it can't be compared with other contexts. In other words, we can only compare assemblages excavated with the same degree of attention: if one pit is excavated with a trowel and sieved, and another with a shovel, their bone assemblages will not be comparable, so their social meaning cannot be accurately contrasted.

We can also note at this point that variation in the legibility of strata is a general property of the buried archaeological resource as a whole. Town sites are in general well stratified, but not always to the same degree in the same town, or even in the same site; in some places strata accumulate; in others they dissipate down slopes. In some places organic material is well preserved; in others, it isn't. Hypothetically we can award points to sites depending on how well preserved the assemblage is and how legible the strata are (Carver 2009, 348). It is a natural tendency of the curious excavator to look harder when they see less. Stratigraphic units, layers, or contexts do not simply exist for all to see and record. They must be defined and the act of definition recorded too.

Similar properties of uncertainty affect the most crucial of all the procedures applied to a well-stratified site: putting the stratigraphic units in order. A section has the weakness of reporting only a very local sequence; but it has the strength of providing a full and permanent record of what the sequence was based on. Those who favor the *schnitt* method also emphasize its checkablity, and feel they are making more objective reports of the stratification than those who order each context one at a time.

Stratigraphy using single-context records (otherwise known as the Harris matrix) places the contexts on a diagram that shows the order in which they were deposited (Harris 1975; 1989; Roskams 2001). There is no doubt that this is a quintessentially useful, even inevitable, method for ordering contexts in well-stratified sites. My published comments about it—sometimes misreported or misunderstood (e.g., Harris et al. 1993, 16; Roskams 2001, 156)— are not that it is wrong (I never said that) but that there are ways of developing the same basic idea that have their uses too. I also think it needs to be acknowledged that you can't make much use of a stratification diagram where there isn't much stratification. Therefore, to demand the adoption of single-context recording everywhere would be absurd, especially where there are no definable contexts. It is my conviction that there is no method that *must* be adopted everywhere. Methods serve designs, not the other way round.

The recording of contexts (including, of course, planning them) and their ordering in a stratification diagram (e.g., a Harris matrix) is an essential but not an adequate record of an archaeological excavation. In scientific terms, it is necessary but not sufficient. This is more than a scholastic assertion, because its sufficiency, or not, determines the cost of archaeology, particularly commercial archaeology, in the field. As the reader will have guessed by now, the purpose of my thesis is to try to connect what we need from excavation with what we know how to discover; this alone determines the price and, thus, the income and the health of our profession.

One way of conceptualizing stratigraphic units to better serve research is as a series of nested sets. If a grain of sand is the smallest thing we can see with the naked eye, we can term it a "component." A set of components, via an act of definition, forms a "context"; a set of contexts forms a "feature"; and a set of features forms a "structure". Each level of definition requires a higher level of interpretation (Carver 2009, 20–22). None of them—neither the component, the context, the feature, nor the structure—"exists" in the sense that it has been corroborated scientifically. Our macro units are all defined by humans, using a kind of measured consensus. We will probably all agree when we can see some sand—and most excavators will be prepared to sign up to visible contexts; those who have seen the kind of associated pit, packing stones, and central mold before will be happy to designate it as a post-pit. Some will want to go further and say it supported a post 6 feet high, others will feel sure it was a replacement, and so on. This is all in the nature of our art or science. If you think the interpretation has flown up out of sight, you can always return to the last interpretation that commanded a reasonable consensus. In this way we create a vocabulary for our subject that works locally, and works further afield if humans there behaved in a similar way. If a set of contexts makes feature, then a set of features may make a structure. It may not—but the fact that it sometimes does gives us the impetus to look for one.

Needless to say, once one accepts that strata can be defined in a conceptual hierarchy like this, it is not too daring to allow these higher-order concepts a say in modeling the sequence. And they are beginning to pop up here and there as excavators strive to answer the question "what happened here" in a more succinct way. Tom Saunders (2004) gathered his contexts into groups and used

45

them to create a "land use diagram," with the groups shown succeeding each other in space and time. Colin Renfrew designed a special sequence diagram for Phylakopi that suited the walls and room-fills that he had (2007, 15–18). At Saddler Street, Durham, in 1974, the stratigraphic diagram took account of a peaty deposit and its middens and posts, to represent the different kinds of stratigraphic relationships and their uncertainties in a multi-conceptual sequence (Carver 1979; FIG. 2.2 gives a more recent example).

One area where a difference of opinion persists is the question of whether higher-order concepts should be defined on site, or only later, as espoused by Steve Roskams (2001, 244). The variants of the Harris matrix introduced in recent years—for example, by Magnar Dalland (1984), Norman Hammond (1991a), Patricia Paice (1991), and Bruce Watson at MoLAS (2004)—all tend to record in single contexts and bunch them together in the post-excavation phase. But there are advantages, and no obvious disadvantages, in addressing this higher-level interpretation on site while you can still see the stuff, and to formalize it in feature and structure records, rather than give an opinion to a video camera. However, I certainly concede that there is an important financial issue here; there is a penalty in time, and therefore cost, in defining and interpreting features on site.

The story so far is that stratified sites can be ordered in exquisite detail—and that we could go even further by enlarging our concepts. Meanwhile, we are still faced with the fact that unstratified sites—sites with no strata, or no strata that are visible—represent by far the majority in all countries where people dig. I don't want to belabor the matter, but it is obvious that in these "flat" sites we need to take special measures to bring anomalies into focus and define them as contexts. In temperate climes this almost invariably means working in a broad area, having a tower to see the site from above, and a plentiful supply of water on site. We also need special measures to put the human activities in order. In the absence of stratification, there are happily other devices for ordering: for example, *alignment*, which reasons that graves or buildings that have a similar orientation were close to one another in time; *assemblage*, where the order in which graves are dug is implied by the order in which grave goods were manufactured; and *composition* of the back-fill contexts. In the famous example from Yeavering, a timber hall had burned down, and Brian Hope-Taylor separated the adjacent graves into three groups: those with no charcoal must have been dug before the fire; those with fresh bits of charcoal were dug straight after it; and those with weathered pellets of char-

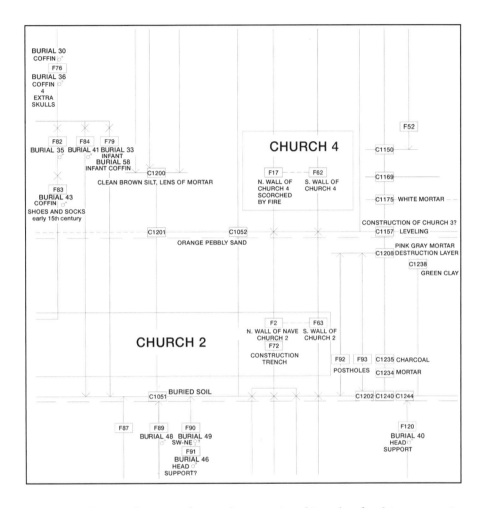

FIGURE 2.2. Stratigraphy: a stratification diagram using a hierarchy of multi-concept units (contexts, features, and structures). Extracted from the diagram of a 1,000-year sequence under the church of St Colman, Portmahomack, Scotland (*diagram by the author/FAS-Heritage*).

coal were dug sometime later (Hope-Taylor 1977, 70, fig. 31). My job here is not to go into all these methods—or the many others—in detail; it is just to emphasize that every site is different, and our approach to defining stratigraphic events and putting them in order should be creative and ingenious, not passive and routine. The task of the field archaeologist is to do what is appropriate, not to do what they always do.

47

## MICRO

Up to now we have been dealing with refinements to conventional storytelling based on the defined context as the lowest common denominator. Now I want to change down a few gears from the macro to the micro, under which heading I include properties that can be targeted, detected, and read on site; but note that these generally refer to things that are scarcely visible, for example, seeds, pollen, and insects. First, it could be useful to introduce on site the idea of the *proxy*, whereby archaeologists detect an activity from objects or features that are not direct evidence for the activity, but imply it, or stand as proxy for it. A straightforward example was provided by Cecily Spall's detection of vellum-working at Portmahomack. She didn't find any vellum or parchment, but she excavated a workshop area with a building, a yard, and a tank; and there she found a curved knife, such as is used in trimming parchment; pumice and rubbing stones for smoothing its surface; much ash containing *spirobis* shells, showing that seaweed had been burned and produced a strongly alkaline compound suitable for tawing; trimmed cattle metapodials; and small round pebbles, which are paralleled in the pegged stretcher-frames of modern parchment makers who use small pebbles to wrap the hides around and prevent them from fraying (Carver and Spall 2004). The connections here are all *inferential*—that is, the individual pieces of data converge on a single likely activity, the making of parchment, without, in this case, actually having recovered any of the product.

Most micro and nano interpretations rely on the proxy idea, and as we'll see, they are flourishing. Some of the earliest advances were made by palaeoecologists, who enriched the assemblages with fragments of plants and insects. At first these were used in an adjectival way—sheep lice implying sheep, for example— but Alan Hall and Harry Kenward realized that the species they identified were signals of something else. Dead insects were proxies for whatever they fed on: the furniture beetle implies furniture. Then they were shown to represent a micro-environment—the dead insects belonging to specifically outdoor or specifically indoor groups. It wasn't only insects that were forming up as silent witnesses to a situation or activity; fragments of plants and animals of particular species were also signs, and when found with artifacts they seem to form repeating sets. Hall and Kenward called these "indicator groups" which pointed to certain crafts— particularly those associated with wool (Hall and Kenward 2003).

Others have taken the idea of indicator packages forward. It has had great success in the Levant, especially by Wendy Matthews at Tell Brak (Matthews et al. 1997) and Çatalhöyük (Matthews 2005), her investigations labeled by the term "microstratigraphy"—in reality, microassemblages. So, beetles associated with camel dung inside houses imply a hearth (burning camel dung) rather than a camel squatting in the front room.

## NANO

Some versions of this kind of "CSI archaeology" (after the TV series *Crime Scene Investigation*) was developed early in connection with human bodies and has been exported to serve the investigation of actual crime scenes, whence the term "forensic" (Cox and Hunter 2005; cf. Sabloff 2008, 97 n. 9). The broader CSI archaeology extends to everything that may have happened on a site, and to tracking back to what happened via the transmogrification from a living organism to a set of inorganic decay products. This field, which I am calling "nano-archaeology," has taken off with tremendous success in the past few years and is pointing a powerful finger towards the future. We are dealing here not with made-up entities like contexts and features, or with sets of microscopic debris discarded in situ. Nano-archaeology operates at a molecular or atomic scale. The elements or molecules that it finds have been absorbed into the deposit from something that was once there. Occasionally that something can be inferred directly; more often, what we find is a proxy for some other material now decayed and vanished.

An early example of nano-excavation was the chemical mapping of the robbed-out burial chamber under Mound 2 at Sutton Hoo in 1988. Previous excavations (see FIG. 1.1) had left an empty tomb with only a few scraps of artifacts, including a number of ship rivets. Effectively the horse had bolted—but that wouldn't have worried Sherlock Holmes, and it didn't worry us. We planned and photographed the sandy chamber floor, which showed a few swirling anomalies, and then swept it with a metal detector, noting the location of ferrous and non-ferrous signals. Then we took 640 30-g samples from the floor and had them analyzed by an inductively coupled plasma (ICP) spectrometer. This reported the amounts contained in each of the "guest" elements present (i.e., not silicon and oxygen). The main response was given by phosphorus and various cations: iron, copper, barium, and calcium. Iron and copper mapped onto forms of anomaly likely to have been artifacts: an iron chain, a bronze cauldron. Another set of elements clustered together at one end—aluminum, strontium, phosphorus, and barium. And we knew from experiments with graves elsewhere at Sutton Hoo that these elements were proxies for the human body (Carver 2005, 58–64). Others have carried this kind of chemical mapping out of the grave and into the settlement, a notable example being the chemical plots inside houses at Çatalhöyük, where calcium-enriched areas implied a plaster floor and the potassium-enriched areas implied ash from hearths (Middleton et al. 2005).

Plots using cations alone have their uses and their perils. Saiano and Scalenghe (2009) proposed that archaeological occupation layers can be detected by signatures of lanthanides even when already mixed into a later soil. But Donald Davidson and others express caution (Wilson et al. 2008): some elements do seem to be reliable proxies for human habitation, whereas others, such as titanium, vanadium, aluminum, and zirconium, showed virtually no correlation with the archaeological remains on the abandoned farms they tested; variations in their concentration were thought to reflect geological differences. But these authors do back barium (Ba), calcium (Ca), copper (Cu), phosphorus (P), lead (Pb), strontium (Sr), and zinc (Zn) as indicators that humans were there. For Oonk and his fellow investigators (2009), the telltale elements were copper, chromium, tin, and neodymium, while depletions of iron and manganese were also found to be universal indicators of human occupation in the house plans. You might think this is all too vague to entrust one's self for a ride. But I think it is a ride worth taking, and one that promises new vistas.

Among the most convincing examples of physico-chemical mapping are those undertaken in Viking houses in Iceland and studied for her Cambridge PhD by Karen Milek, now in post at Aberdeen (2006). The problem with this kind of building (as many Scottish excavators will know) is that while they were once large and imposing, by the time we get to them there appears to be little left. Turf is among the implied building materials. But although it rots away completely, it ought to leave iron-enriched microstrata, which are then very hard to displace. Other immovable decay products should be present too—in fact, as Milek says, minute residues actually have a much better chance of remaining in situ than bones or artifacts, which get dispersed by animals and humans. Drawing on earlier ideas from Helen Smith and others (2001), Milek applied a number of remote sensing techniques to the excavated floor surface of House G excavated at Hofstaðir (FIG. 2.3). These were micromorphology, mapping elements with ICP (see above), acidity, testing for organic matter with LoI (loss on ignition), magnetic susceptibility, and electrical conductivity. These report different physical or chemical properties, which imply materials, which in turn imply activities. In other words, a kind of proxy chain leads back from what has stayed in the soil to what was mostly done in different parts of the house. In the southwest corner we have sodium and magnesium, suggesting seawater, seaweed, or urine, plus high electrical conductivity; overall this is read as an alkaline solution (lye) used in the washing and degreasing of wool. Along the east aisle there were articulated phytoliths in dark grayish brown organic silts, implying compacted grass; zinc, barium, strontium, copper, and nickel suggesting organic matter; and unburnt bone, fragments of pumice, and jasper lying on either side. Interpretation: a grassy bed, sat on to chew bones and work stone. This approach is perhaps even more significant than its results: it treats the house like a complex organism, not just to be sliced or dissected into contexts, but to be examined with a battery of sensors: to be interrogated for its memories.

Magnetic susceptibility, colloquially *mag sus*, was among the methods deployed by Karen Milek. We are used to seeing it trundling along the surface to produce geophysical surveys—but magnetic methods may also be used on excavation sites to resolve questions about strata we can't see. Andy Herries is somewhat of a magnetic champion and has had notable success applying magnetic

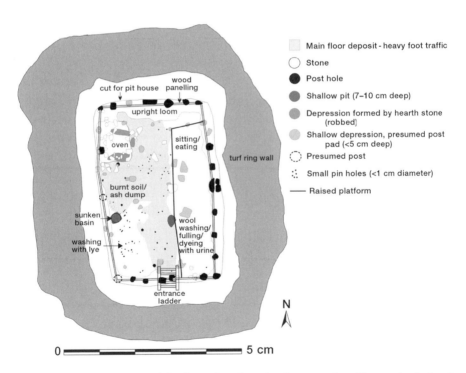

FIGURE 2.3. Interpretation of the floor of a Viking Age house explored by geophysical and geochemical mapping (House G at Hofstaðir, in Mývatnssveit, northeast Iceland) (from Milek 2006, 297, revised February 2011; *courtesy of Karen Milek*).

methods in cave sites, as at Pinnacle Point in South Africa. Among the mass of opaque strata, mag sus can distinguish hearths, archaeological strata of the Middle Stone Age, and later colluvium, each with its own magnetic signature. Hearths can be distinguished from random groups of stones by magnetic alignment: stones found together with the same magnetic alignment had all been heated up together and so constitute a hearth. Ochre, the palaeolithic coloring of choice, is also highly magnetic, and its magnetic properties differ from source to source; the source can thus be determined. Lastly, the mag sus readings of layers vary with rainfall and can be aligned with oxygen isotope periods to give an approximate date. So a sequence of climate, activities, and imported materials in an occupied cave can be determined by means of this instrument alone (Herries 2009; see also p. 93).

## PROTEOMICS

Lipids—that is, the insoluble decay products of organic compounds—were first extracted from the walls of pots, where they were used to identify what the pots had originally contained—for example, milk or wine (Evershed et al. 2001). In a 2009 paper, B. Hjulstro and S. Isaksson added lipids to the range of parameters detectable in strata on site. They plotted the organic traces on the floor of a reconstructed house at Lejhre in Denmark, noting areas enriched with coprostanol and 24-ethylcoprostanol, compounds that could be directly associated with "faecal biomarkers for herbivores"—or, in ordinary-person-speak, cowpats. In other words, the biomarkers showed where cows were stalled.

Organic molecules, the stuff of life, and their proxies, are very much the targets of the new frontier. Don Brothwell's current European Research Council project at the University of York aims to develop skills in detecting residues in human burials—from the body itself, stuff that it ingested, and materials applied to the body, such as embalming fluids (pers. comm.). He is using the methods of micromorphology, scanning electron microscopy (SEM), energy dispersive X-ray spectroscopy (EDX), microprobes, chromatography, and mass spectrometry to discover decay products in graves at the macro, micro, and nano levels; for example, resins, spices, waxes, gums, bitumen, fats, and oils can be deduced from terpenoids, alkanes, hopanes, and sterols, each with its diagnostic molecular structures. In a pilot study on two Yemen cliff burials, Brothwell claims to have detected proxies for skin, hair, uric acid, and cholesterol (pers. comm.). These techniques may also find a use in modern forensic medicine—for example, by posthumously detecting drug use. A paper in 2009 reported the extraction of alkaloids of mind-altering *Banisteriopsis* from mummies in the Azapa Valley in the Andes, an area otherwise known for its graves containing tubes and "snuffing tablets" (Ogalde et al. 2009).

Investigators in pursuit of proteins, or *proteomics*, are flexing their muscles. Proteomics has been used to identify fish processing from traces on 30 flint artifacts from an Early Neolithic TRB site in south Sweden; here there was a correlation between fish protein and use-wear analysis (Högberg et al. 2009). A new target is to identify the species involved, and this is in sight. Animals usually leave lots of bone—but on some sites, the bone has gone, was never much there, or is otherwise barely detectable. ZOOMS is a zoology mass spectrometry project directed by Matthew Collins (also of the University of York) that aims to distinguish the collagen of different animals from miniscule samples. Collagen is a protein consisting of 3,000 amino acids, which together provide a signature of the animal species. It is protected underground by being bound in fibrils and trapped in the lattice of the bone apatite. It can last up to 1.5 million years (so far). But it melts at 36 °C and is eroded in hot, and especially hot and wet, soils. The collagen chain consists of repeating subchains of peptides of standard length. The weight of each peptide depends on the amino acids present in the subchain. So the peptide has a mass typical of its amino acids and, thus, of the animal species. Starting from a tiny crumb, then, not only can we tell a camel from a rabbit, but we can at last distinguish a sheep from a goat.

I need to mention two of the most exciting kinds of molecular investigation, stable isotopes and DNA, although both currently present us field archaeologists with a number of problems. Carbon and nitrogen isotopes give an indication of diet, while strontium and oxygen isotopes are used to detect "foreigners" in cemeteries, since their signatures vary with ground water and get into the childhood teeth. There are numerous examples of successful analyses from Europe to South Africa (Sealy 2001; Linderholm et al. 2008; Müldner et al. 2009). But since these inquiries feed off individual human bones and teeth, they require lots of samples to sustain a generalized historical argument—such as the case for migration or invasion. The method does not itself influence the amount of destructive excavation that's done, except perhaps to increase it; we do have some enormous reserves of material, such as the 2,000 cremations and inhumations at Spong Hill (see Chapter 1, p. 20), where a large-scale census of the origins of a population may one day be undertaken.

DNA characterizes analysis for human and animal remains down to an individual, but still works best on modern samples. In this, it is useful in pointing to what will eventually be possible. For example, a recent plot of DNA samples extracted from 3,000 modern Europeans offered a clear correlation between DNA and birthplace, implying that the study of migration can at last move away from the realm of politicized speculation (Novembre et al. 2008). However, as with stable isotopes, the quantities needed for a convincing generalization are very large.

Ancient DNA (aDNA) is really what we want, because archaeologists don't want to make any *assumptions* about the way people may be related—we want to find it out. But aDNA does not survive in hot climates and is destroyed by most recovery and storage schemes (C. Smith et al. 2003; Pruvost 2007). DNA samples are also notoriously susceptible to contamination; modern DNA is picked up from the highly obtrusive biosphere in which field archaeologists themselves work. It is against this background that we should consider the results of the investigation known as *The Farm beneath the Sand* that was published in 2009. From previous findings of plant and animal DNA in Siberia, North America, and New Zealand, Martin Hebsgaard and his colleagues argued that aDNA in soil is less subject to degradation and leaching in cool conditions, and quickly binds onto clays and sand and organo-mineral complexes. Thus aDNA in soil—or dirt aDNA (adDNA)—does survive and need not move much (Hebsgaard et al. 2009). Their target site was a Norse settlement in Greenland dating between AD 1000 and 1400, which had been excavated in 1992 from beneath 1.5 m of sand and gravel. The faunal and insect records had indicated that the farm itself had not been occupied continuously, although the fields around had been grazed virtually non-stop. Thus there was a control on the DNA experiment, which took place in a field adjacent to the excavated settlement.

A small trench was cut through layers of peat interleaved with sand about 50 m from the buildings, and samples were taken from the section with a hollow pipe. The seven cores were sealed and frozen and taken to laboratories in Copenhagen and Murdoch, Australia, via Canada. The surface of the samples was spiked with a known DNA molecule to check whether it had penetrated into the inner core during handling. Then the DNA in the inner cores was amplified using the PCR (polymerase chain reaction) method, and sequenced. The sequence of bases then gave the most likely animal present. Parallel cores were used to provide AMS (accelerator mass spectrometry) radiocarbon dates from layers of peat.

The chief species present in the inner cores were cattle, sheep, goat, mouse, reindeer, and human. The humans were disregarded, being a likely contaminant; for the animals, both the species and their quantities were considered representative. It was found that sheep and cattle arrived together around AD 1040; but while the sheep population remained steady, the cattle population fluctuated—high–low, high–low. Both species declined from ca. 1365 and had disappeared by 1520 (FIG. 2.4).

These results correlate well with the excavated sequence and its bone record and raise confidence that the samples tell a story, without too much distortion from leaching or contamination. The project showed that DNA survival does not need permafrost, but can remain representative in temperate and wet conditions. In other words, there's no reason why it should not work in most northern countries. Of course, this adDNA reported a general presence from urine and faeces, rather than the use of specific animals (as reported by the bone record). But it's a start. The sequence provided by The Farm beneath the Sand is exciting since it implies that the history of the world can be explored by a scientist with an auger, locality by locality. However, history is

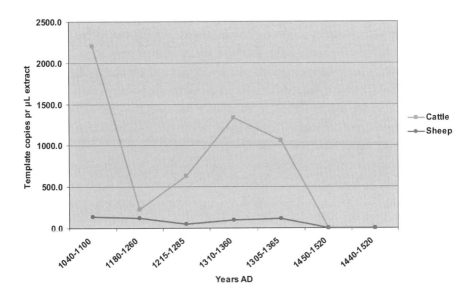

FIGURE 2.4. Fluctuations in the quantities of cattle *(top line)* and sheep DNA as recorded in a core taken beside a Viking-period site, The Farm beneath the Sand, 80 km east of Nuuk. These data reflect the arrival and emphasis of farming and its eventual disappearance at one point on the coast of Greenland (Hebsgaard et al. 2009, fig. 5; *courtesy of Martin Hebsgaard and* Antiquity).

not just a general sequence, but many interwoven narratives. Soil DNA joins the toolbox, but mainly in the service of environmental and agronomic change.

## REMOTE EXCAVATION

What we are seeing in this cursory review of nano-archaeology is the way that landscape methods are invading site survey, and site survey methods are joining the excavation team. Stages of investigation are now no longer separated by their tools, as with survey, prospection, and excavation, but by their purpose: reconnaissance, evaluation, dissection (see Chapter 5). We have already seen that mag sus is discovering properties in strata way beyond simply noting that something is there. We know that ground-penetrating radar also reports more than we can so far understand. It can also report data in time slices—that is, anomalies encountered at different depths. Lawrence Conyers' 2010 article shows how radar can find the slope of the principal occupation surfaces and remap the anomalies onto them, offering the changing geography of a site, as in the case of a Nabataean garden in Petra (Conyers 2010, 183). On-site remote mapping is where the future lies. As we get to know the underground world better, the power of nano-investigation will operate a pincer movement on the old dig-and-write mentality. Our methods will be less muscular, but our stories more interesting.

Radar reads interfaces, especially in nice dry sites, where the radiation doesn't get attenuated. Our nano methods so far entail taking readings directly under ground; that is, we dig, sample, and then infer the invisible part of the assemblage. Could we ever get to the point where we can not only map underground, without going there, like radar, but identify elements, molecules, and materials—all the components of contexts—and do it without sampling? Two instruments already in use suggest that this idea is not so farfetched and might even be just around the corner. The IR (infrared) gun works by distinguishing different organic materials that return different reflections from IR light. The IR gun has been used in Sweden to find organics by simply pointing it at a section. It recognizes bone, textiles, and vitamin C from fruit (http://www.polychromix.com/). The XRF (X-ray fluorescence) gun can determine the presence of copper and silver in possible workshop debris. It has been used, for example, by N. Kato, I. Nakai, and Y. Shindo at Raya port (8th to 12th centuries) on the Sinai Peninsula to distinguish two types of Islamic glass: glass vessels with low titanium and iron and high strontium, which were probably produced in the Syria–Palestine region in the 8th century; and samples with high levels of calcium, titanium, and iron, probably produced in Egypt in the 8th century (*http://socarchsci.blogspot.com/2009/06/handheld-xrf-and-archaeology.html*). Having the instrument on site gives you the chance to map surface sherds and thus distinguish the workshop areas of the two periods, and to test assemblages as you go along, rather than wait until the later post-excavation program off site when nothing remains to be checked.

It seems little short of miraculous that these gadgets can read off the presence of specific atoms and complex molecules by waving them above a surface, like reading a bar code. Will there be a time when they could operate remotely? To some extent they already do, and that time will come more quickly if we want it to.

## CONCLUSION

So should we? I believe it is important to embrace and develop this kind of technology for two quite urgent purposes. The first is in the service of *evaluation*. There has been a huge improvement seen over the past 30 years in predictive deposit mapping; but it still isn't good enough to put a clear value on an archaeological site in advance of its redevelopment, and most evaluation projects resort pretty quickly to test pits and trenches—"just to be sure." Part of the new prescription to be laid out in Chapter 6 requires greater confidence in the instruments, with an appreciation of what they can do; and to pass our own convictions onto our collaborating professions. At the present time, it would be a rash planner who withheld planning permission just on the basis of a radar plot. But confidence could come if there were more remote sensing studies of sites, which were published after excavation. If the predictive mapping also showed the old water mains, cellars, and foundations with convincing clarity, there would be a better chance of accepting such images as a basis for making decisions about building and about research opportunities.

The second urgent purpose concerns sites that are not threatened but are not available for research either because of stringent conservation policies. We shall need to come back to this too (p. 137)—but let's just observe here that remote mapping is no longer about finding sites, but about studying them. My very brief review of technology-in-the-making, brought together from many different sources, shows that given sufficient ingenuity and R&D, even the most sacred places—like Stonehenge—could be studied in depth without digging an irreverent and irreversible hole in the middle of it (cf. Pitts 2009).

The journey we just undertook from mega to nano was intended also to broaden the concept of an archaeological deposit and to convince you that it deserves much more than the same, single response each time. The "context" is not a unit of human activity; it is a macroscopic unit of strata, defined by an archaeologist using its color and texture. Occasionally its interfaces are nice and clear. But mostly they aren't. Clear or not, the context represents only one set of macroscopic properties, and perhaps not the determinant one. Context-only recording is inadequate. Interpretation "at the trowels' edge" (Chapter 1, p. 24) is only a tithe of the interpretations that are possible: necessary but not sufficient. When we can, contexts need to be resolved into higher-concept families, features, and interpretive ideas that express human actions—paths, pits, floors, walls, and graves. These features form patterns too, which show concepts of still higher-order cognition—a structure, a ritual space, a kin-group.

The context also needs to be deconstructed beyond its macroscopic components, to reveal its microchemical and microbiological properties—because so much lies hidden there. These diagnostic properties do not necessarily map into the context. Urinating cattle create an intrusive context of their own, spread untidily through a space. And yet this invisible context marks a byre.

It can be seen that this multi-concept, multi-technique deconstruction of an archaeological deposit is taking archaeological investigation into the intellectual forum of the arts through the media of the sciences. Our inquiries will serve historical, processual, and cognitive goals equally well. Archaeological investigation does not exist independently from what it wants to find out. But once mapped out in the design phase, it can proceed using its own logic. The new technology is thus re-arming the objectives of archaeological research, in ways that we have yet to appreciate. In some ways, research needs to catch up with what archaeological fieldwork can now do.

If this transition continues, excavation could, or should, be transformed from a hearty shoveling exercise on a building site to something closer to a crime scene investigation, with strong laboratory backing. We would see a transition in the appearance of the workforce from donkey jacket to white lab-coat. There could be a corresponding improvement in the way archaeologists are regarded and the amount they are paid. In the commercial sector this transformation is much needed. But these matters do not only depend on science per se, but with the way archaeology is procured or purchased by society—and what society wants us for. These are the things that make archaeology the career it is and influence the career it should be. This is embedded in the social context in which we work, the subject of the next chapter.

# CHAPTER 3

# ON THE STREET:

# ARCHAEOLOGISTS AND SOCIETY

### THREE WINDOWS: VIKING DUBLIN, AFRICAN BROADWAY, GOLDEN VILLAGE

Wood Quay is a site on the banks of the River Liffey in Dublin where the Vikings had built a shanty town and waterfront in the 10th century AD. When rediscovered in the 20th century, it was found to have preserved its timber houses, jetties, boat parts, and light industries very well. It was an abandoned wooden conurbation, rich in organic artifacts, bones, and debris. The site was purchased in 1974 by Dublin Corporation, who planned to build themselves a fine new headquarters there; and recognizing the archaeological interest, they cleared the site and invited the National Museum of Ireland (NMI) to carry out some excavations. By 1976 the NMI had run out of money, which suited Dublin Corporation since they were anxious to get on with their building. But the excavation was far from finished, and tension rose between the museum and the corporation. The historical value of the site was championed by the Friends of Medieval Dublin, who campaigned for more excavation and for the conservation of earthworks that could still be seen. They soon acquired a powerful advocate in Father Xavier Martin, a Jesuit priest, who took the campaign to the courts in Ireland and then Europe, protected from financial penalty by the convenient measure of having taken a vow of poverty.

In 1977, Father Martin was granted an injunction in the Irish courts prohibiting further damage to the medieval earthworks, and in 1978 Mr. Justice Hamilton declared the site a National Monument. Strangely, however, this only gave it another six weeks of excavation, so the Friends collected 210,000 signatures on a petition, and 20,000 people took to the streets and marched through Dublin, with banners demanding "Save Wood Quay" (FIG. 3.1). Ultimately, however, the movement was unsuccessful and the forces of development overpowered it. In March 1979, a second injunction from Father Martin failed, and the bulldozers moved in (Heffernan 1988).

This celebrated case is a useful one since it shows something of what citizens want from archaeology. It wasn't conservationist—they wanted the site dug, not conserved; it wasn't nationalist—the people being dug up were mostly not Celts, but Norwegians. What this population of Dubliners wanted was good quality research—research that took as long as it took and told us what it told us. They were campaigning for the right to know.

Now let's switch the scene to New York City 20 years later, specifically to Manhattan and 290 Broadway. At this site, another large government body, the General Services Agency (GSA), planned to build a headquarters intended, ironically, for the federal Environmental Protection Agency. Aware of a possible impact on cultural resources, in 1989 GSA executed a memorandum of

FIGURE 3.1. Demonstrators urging further excavation at Wood Quay, Dublin, in March 1979 (*photo by Peter Thursfield; courtesy of* The Irish Times).

agreement with the Advisory Council on Historic Preservation and the New York City Landmarks Preservation Commission. They commissioned an impact statement, using the archaeological contractor Historic Conservation and Interpretation (HCI). HCI noted the former presence on the 1755 Maerschalck map of a "Negro Burial Ground" which you might think would set the alarm bells ringing. However, they assessed that little of this burial ground would remain, so GSA bought the site and proceeded to dig the foundations for their 34-story tower, with its adjacent pavilion. They didn't need planning permission, being the government, and they didn't consult the people of Harlem because "the site wasn't in Harlem."

Monitoring the site in 1991, HCI discovered articulated skeletons under 25 feet of fill and commenced excavation with another firm, Metropolitan Forensic Archaeology Team (MFAT). At the end of the year, GSA held a press conference to announce the discovery, raising considerable disquiet among the African-American community. Mayor David Dinkins took up the cause, pressure mounted on GSA to stop the building, and the archaeologists were working ten to twelve hours a day, seven days a week, to remove the skeletons—and remove the problem. Meanwhile, the builders also hit human remains and were spotted attempting to spirit them off the site in skips. The word got out and the local newspaper, Greenwich's *Village Voice*, had a field day. The mayor came down to look and demanded to see the archaeological research design. It seemed there wasn't one. And this led to Laurie Beckelmann's famous aphorism expressed at the congressional hearing: "Any archaeological excavation is useless without a research design. . . . It's like driving a car in a foreign country without a road map or destination."

In July 1992, a congressional subcommittee demanded that excavation be stopped as a sign of respect, and in October President Bush signed Public Law 102-393, requiring construction to cease and approving $3 million to make a memorial. A research laboratory was set up by new archaeological contractors John Milner Associates (JMA) at 6 World Trade Center, where the excavation was written up and exhibitions were held, generating tremendous emotion and sympathy for the plight of the New York slaves of 200 years before—an effective historical as well as political exposure.

But that wasn't quite the end of the story. In an article entitled "Black Bones, White Science," *The Village Voice* described the tug-of-war between rivals for the post-excavation contract. JMA and MFAT each had data sheets relating to some of the 400 burials. MFAT gave copies of theirs to JMA who did not reciprocate, and in a "lunchtime raid," copies of the JMA records were removed from the World Trade Center lab for copying. In principle, both organizations could now publish.

In the end, the project and its records were handed over to Professor Michael Blakey of Howard University, who had issued an alternative research design. I met him on a visit to the site in 1993 and heard how he was going to use the latest scientific procedures to study the details of the African diaspora, locate the origins of the people who had arrived in the 18th century as slaves, their state of health, whether it got better or worse, their forms of worship, their communities—in brief, the whole story. The site itself subsequently became a National Landmark and memorial of honor for these, some of New York's most significant but underdocumented citizens (FIG. 3.2; Blakey 2001; documentation summarized in Carver 2003, 7–13; King 2005, 35, compares this project with the better-ordered Five Points, also in New York; Sabloff 2008, 96; see now *http://www.nps.gov/afbg/index.htm* and *http://www.africanburialground.gov /ABG_Main.htm*; interview with Michael Blakey at *http://www.archaeology. org/online/interviews/blakey/index.html*).

The battle here was focused on respect rather than new knowledge, but digging up history was very much on the agenda. Politics naturally packed a bigger punch than research on a very expensive piece of real estate; and yet it was historical research that provided the hard currency of the argument. As in Dublin, the popular demand here was for good research, and research in which the modern social context was acknowledged and respected. People care about the way the past is used, but they don't necessarily have an axe to grind. Everyone, in and out of Harlem, in and out of Manhattan, had a right to see what was proposed in advance in the form of a project design—not just what sort of a building was going up, but how it was proposed to handle the historical roots of the site.

A third story takes us forward another 20 years and into Cambodia. In 2006, members of the University of Phnom Penh conducting surveys of Iron Age sites came across extensive looting at the appropriately named village of Bit Meas ("gold plated"). Large areas riddled with pits showed where looters had pillaged furnished graves (FIG. 3.3a). The following year, the plundering had moved to neighboring Prohear, where it was encountered by archaeology students Vin Laychour and Seng Sonetra; they sent an emotional email to their former German professor, who in turn contacted Andreas Reinecke, an active academic and fieldworker. Reinecke took up the cause and for the next nine months raised money and obtained permissions for a scientific excavation of

FIGURE 3.2. The memorial at the site of the African Burial Ground, excavated in 1993 (*photo by Brian Boyd, reproduced with his permission*).

what was left of the Prohear Iron Age cemetery. During this time the villagers had reduced an area as big as two football pitches to a battlefield of craters. It had produced a mass of gold objects and at least 20 Dong Son drums, most sold as scrap metal at the going rate of US 20 cents a kilo, and probably laundered by dealers at profits of many hundred times that figure.

When the archaeological team arrived in February 2008, new houses had gone up everywhere, thanks to the villagers' windfall wealth. Nothing was left of the cemetery except for what was still under the road, and even here the local looters had begun tunneling beneath. This was the area that Reinecke got permission to dig. The villagers wanted to dig it for themselves and were reluctant to accept the concept that the past was not going to profit them; but they did get a new road. The first task was thus to persuade the community that archaeological investigation was a new and better way of proceeding, even if the benefits were less tangible. Public meetings were held, in which archaeologists, officials, and their interpreters weighed and balanced the relative influences of individual profit, administrative coercion, investment, fame, heritage, and historical knowledge.

FIGURE 3.3. Rescue in Cambodia. (*a*): Looters active at the Iron Age site of Bit Meas, Cambodia in 2006. (*b*): Programmed archaeological excavation under the road at Prohear, Cambodia (Reinecke et al. 2009, 20, 40; *courtesy of Andreas Reinecke*).

From then on, the story of Prohear becomes really uplifting. Once they knew there was nothing to fear, the previous "specialists" came forward one by one to share their considerable knowledge about how to find graves and to anticipate what was in them. The star digger was villager Kong Sung, who had been credited with seven Dong Son drum finds and had bought himself a water buffalo with the proceeds. Although 50% of the archaeology under the road had been already been tunneled away, Reinecke impressed the local community and the visitors with the great care he took and the reverence he showed (FIG. 3.3b). He swiftly published a beautifully illustrated book, which explains what he did, what the scientific analyses showed and how they work, as well as what it is all for and why it matters (Reinecke et al. 2009). In brief, he not only won the opportunity to do research, he won the hearts and minds of the looters; in effect, he won the argument.

These three anecdotes introduce questions that are important for the health and survival of our profession. Where do we fit in? Do the public want what we offer, and are they prepared to pay? Or is it only government that can dispense taxpayers' money, altruistically, to compile a portfolio of the past? Our task is to define what is worth paying for, our *product*, since our relationship with the rest of society depends on that. If we offer ourselves for hire on a false premise, the public will eventually discover it.

Our case studies endorse the general necessity of the preservation of the past and demand that it should be exploited only for public benefit, as heritage. Each of the countries we discussed had heritage legislation, and this was based to various degrees on the idea of the past as property, and state property in particular. Clearly such legislation had failed. The loss of public property was not what had got the protesters onto the streets, or stopped them from looting. They did not demand the preservation of a nationally important monument. On the contrary, they demanded the excavation of the sites in question—but only in the name of science. They were not inclined to regard an archaeological site as property at all—but as a source of knowledge—and that knowledge was the entitlement of all. Knowledge is not, it seems, the private property of an intellectual elite, as some politicians like to make out; rather, the hunger for knowledge is part of the human makeup; we are curiosity-driven animals. Exploration of the unknown is ultimately what archaeologists have to sell.

Note also that for the public, the besetting sin of the archaeologists as well as the governments was an inability to predict what was there and plan for it. David Dinkins, the black mayor of New York, did not object to the excavation of the slave cemetery—provided it was done with respect; he objected to the fact that there was no published project design. And insofar as there was a plan, it didn't consult the people of Harlem. A project design can never be complete unless it takes account of the social context of the project. And the social context is what concerns us here.

## WHAT SORT OF STATE ARE YOU IN?

If governments represent and control people, which is presumably what they are for, the ambience they create for archaeology depends on the type of state concerned (TABLE 3.1). Some states see archaeology as purely recreational, like angling. Perhaps there needs to be a bit of conservation, otherwise fish stocks in rivers will run out. But on the whole, this is a leisure activity that regulates itself. I would call this type of regime *unregulated*; it is how Britain was before Pitt-Rivers came along.

Other governments see archaeology as a national asset, with results that belong to the nation as a whole. The government is the custodian of the soul of the nation and principal funder of research in the historical sciences. This

Table 3.1. Archaeological procurement in three different kinds of political system

| TYPE OF REGIME | UNREGULATED | REGULATED | DEREGULATED |
|---|---|---|---|
| *Source of finance* | Trusts, charities | State | Developer |
| *Method of procurement* | Ad hoc | State program Media pressure | Planning system Planning consultants Curators' specs |
| *Who does the fieldwork?* | Volunteers, students, directed by individual researcher | Laborers, directed by Inspector | Archaeological contractor Professional excavators |
| *Research output* | Peer pressure Depends on the individual | Depends on government priorities | [Not part of contract] |
| *Quality control* | Peer-group | Inspectors Licenses | Consultants (?) |

Source: Carver 2009, 366; *courtesy of the author/FAS-Heritage*

kind of regime is *regulated*. All archaeology is looked after and done by the government, or carried out on its behalf by agencies, the universities, and academies of science. Everything, including rescue, is paid for by taxes. This has been the principal mode in Eastern Europe, and to some extent in Western Europe too. Here and there, archaeologists still hanker after the perceived security of state centralization—for example, in France, Scandinavia, and Scotland.

The third kind of regime is one more familiar in England and the United States. It is partially regulated, but delegates archaeological work to the private sector. This work is generally administered through two different government ministries; one (concerned with education) funds research through universities, and the other (concerned with the environment) manages the resources and monitors mitigation through the planning system, paid for by developers. Thus *deregulated* countries have two government departments supporting two archaeology professions that rely on different funding and principles and have become dangerously separated.

Let's stay with the deregulated system, because although it is presently in the minority among governments, there is a strong possibility that it will eventually inherit the earth. The basic control mechanism is still to treat cultural resources as property, something for which there is already plenty of legislation. Cultural property is property belonging to a nation, to be protected unless the government allows its use, the government being synonymous with the nation. Early legislation in Britain and the United States focused on drawing up lists or *schedules* of these properties and then, from the 1970s, began to add prescriptions for dealing with their loss through looting and development. In 1966 the US government passed the National Historic Preservation Act, with a National Register of Historic Places. A site was placed on the register if it had historic significance—and vice versa. *Section 106* of the act provided for the conservation by recording of a threatened site that could be shown to be significant, at the expense of the site's developer. The act is administered by each state through a State Historic Preservation Office or SHPO (colloquially known as "shippo"). It took the UK another 25 years to catch up with this idea, except that they did not introduce SHPOs with their 1990 reforms (see p. 77). This was a pity, since compared with county archaeologists, SHPOs have considerable control over the development process. In 1990, with the introduction of the Native American Graves Protection and Repatriation Act (NAGPRA), the United States took a major step in recognizing the right of descendant communities to reclaim and dispose of human remains in their ancestral territories, appointing THPOs (colloquially "trippos"), Tribal Historic Preservation Officers, to oversee fair play (Neumann and Sanford 2001).

This legislative package drives the whole enormous cultural resource management (CRM) industry in the United States; thus the activity is known as "Section 106 archaeology" or "compliance archaeology," "CRM archaeology," and so forth. Such prescriptions, paralleled in many countries, serve public interests in a particular way. They start from a recognition of physical assets, standing or buried, and treat them as resources to be managed. The two main preoccupations of management are the protection or *conservation* of the assets for the future, and *mitigation*, the recording of the assets when they have to be sacrificed in the name of social or economic progress.

In the United States, as in other countries, this legislation underpins the greater part of all archaeological investigation. The proportion of archaeologists living off mitigation projects is perhaps now 80% or more of the total practitioners of archaeology. It is important to appreciate what kind of archaeology gets done as a result. It is obvious that the logic of "manage, protect, and mitigate" is not that of our demonstrators on the streets, who wanted knowledge, not conserved cultural property; nor is it what most archaeologists themselves want out of archaeology. They too are in it to know more. There is thus a contradiction between what archaeologists want to do and the economic justification for paying them.

## THE GOOD, THE BAD, AND THE GRUMPY

This is an important, if inconvenient fact. Archaeologists generally begin as volunteers or students, unpaid but fed and looked after by staff who train and cosset them. They get to shoulder responsibilities on site, often indecently soon, and are party to the design and subsequent interpretations and decisions on a site on a daily basis. A small fraction of these students go on to become university lecturers who continue thinking that archaeology is always like that—lots of fun, booze, sex, tents, and troweling.

However, of those who stay in the business, the vast majority go into government or commercial outfits, the CRM sector. The activities of CRM archaeologists depend on who is paying them to do what, something that many prefer to forget. There are three main ways of being paid to do archaeology outside the university: as a government employee, as conscripted labor, and as an employee in a private company. Government and local government employees work in archaeology and for archaeology but within the legislation

68

that employs them; thus they did once excavate, but now do a lot of administrative casework and monument inspection; but they may cause excavations to happen or succeed in preventing them.

In the early days of mitigation, the government paid field archaeologists through conscription schemes. Famously, under the WPA, the Work Program Administration, the Tennessee Valley Authority in the 1930s used a mass of conscript labor to excavate sites under threat from dam construction (see, e.g., Wendorf and Thompson 2002). The director was William Webb, a physics professor, who devised schemes of recording that reported findings in a standardized scientific way and established the "feature" as the primary unit of archaeological significance. The success of this project led to others, such as the Missouri River Basin Program, recording historic sequences in advance of flooding after the war. Governments also noted that this was a handy way of dealing with unemployment, so it has been reactivated in various ways since then. Like many other archaeologists in the United Kingdom in the 1970s and 1980s, I ran Manpower Services Commission (MSC) schemes in which job-seekers were temporarily employed by universities and trusts undertaking large-scale excavations. Conveniently, the archaeological mood in Britain was at that time intellectually much in favor of "total" excavations, believing them to be more revealing than those that were targeted. Thus, huge areas were excavated by teams that were supervised and paid but non-professional in character. Whole cemeteries, villages, and town sites were unearthed, and many eventually appeared in print. Work at Wasperton, where 12 contiguous hectares were excavated, opened up a whole landscape stretching from the Neolithic to the 7th century AD. The publication of its cemetery was achieved in 2009, 29 years after it was dug, and the Roman phase is still laboring on. At Stafford, three large areas of a town were successfully excavated by a crew with an average age of 17, funded by a YOP (Youth Opportunities Programme). For some of the recruits, this was an apprenticeship that led on to employment as a fully fledged professional—not an unpleasant experience and not a bad outcome. A spectrum of modern archaeological participants may be seen in FIGURE 3.4a–f.

The way people have entered the field archaeology profession undoubtedly tempers their subsequent view of it, something worth bearing in mind as we examine its current condition. There is naturally a huge chasm between those who, from a long preparation on icy acres of gravel, have arrived in employment and feel themselves lucky to be paid for engaging in one of life's most exciting activities, and those who entered the profession thinking it already was one,

a

b

FIGURE 3.4. Field archaeology players: (*a*): Visitors to a rescue site in the middle of a rubbish tip, Italy; (*b*): Volunteers moving a dirt pile (*photos by the author/FAS-Heritage*).

c

d

FIGURE 3.4. (*cont.*) Field archaeology players: (*c*): trainees on site; (*d*): metal detectorist assisting on an excavation (*photos by the author/FAS-Heritage*). (*Continued on next page*)

e

FIGURE 3.4. (*cont.*) Field archaeology players: (*e*): professional recording a test trench for evaluation; (*f*): professionals testing chemically contaminated strata (*photos by the author/FAS-Heritage*).

f

and have continually looked inward at their own status. In the 1980s, as China was beginning to make contacts with the West, I hosted the then head of the Bureau of Cultural Relics at Beijing, Guo Zhan, who was on a tour of Britain and had no doubt come to see our Wall (i.e., Hadrian's). Over a horn or two of excessively strong *baijiu*, we fell to discussing our relative conceptions of the archaeologist in society. We had common ground on the primacy of research, and the centralization practiced in China was generally beneficial to it. But how had he coped with the Cultural Revolution? He was surprisingly open in his answer. It had been very bad for many academics: a loss of status and of earnings, sometimes permanent. But for archaeologists, it had been often rather inspiring. Inspiring? Yes: he had been sent to inner Mongolia to work as a shepherd. For research into early agriculture this proved intensely interesting; studying pastoralism in a library was one thing, looking after sheep quite another. This is not to say that the Cultural Revolution was a healthy shake-up for archaeologists; only that professionalism in archaeology needs to be regarded with a sense of proportion.

Nearly all commercial field archaeologists nowadays work for companies and have an uncertain sense of their status—if we are to judge from recent literature. The recurrent resentments center on lack of security, lack of career structure, lack of respect, and lack of money. This does not make for a very creative industry. Let's look at two recent manifesto statements. In their *American Antiquity* article of 2003, Ian Hodder and Åsa Berggren assign a reduced intellectual status to professional fieldworkers, who suffer by being separated from their universities and apparently have no voice in the interpretation of their sites. They see this as descendant from the old antiquary-laborer system, and blame the class system, then and now. Their remedy is "reflexive archaeology," a rubric that covers the recording of individual contexts and the construction and promulgation of individual site narratives or monologues. To quote them: "Reflexive archaeology" provides "systematic opportunities for field archaeologists to engage in narrative construction and to provide critique of those narratives in relation to data and social context" (Berggren and Hodder 2003, 426). The act of observation and recording is portrayed as demeaning and the act of interpretation as uplifting. "The old theoretical debate about the separation between data and interpretation in archaeology partly has a social basis. It is not an abstract philosophical discussion. It is about who is empowered to interpret. And on the whole the answer has been "not the excavator" (Berggren and Hodder 2003, 425).

It is hard to recognize the social basis of this report, which appears to emanate from the planet Zog. Commercial archaeologists are not deprived of research by having the wrong theory or being subject to some abstruse relic of the class war. They are just not paid to do it. Of course, being archaeologists, that doesn't stop them from trying, and they do succeed, particularly in the recording and interpretation of what is found on site, something every professional field-worker does and always has done. Nor is there any evidence that excavators and recorders find their role on site demeaning. In science one receives as much kudos for being at the work face in the lab as for designing and supervising projects, and the idea that the outcome is not shared is baffling. I am glad I escaped working on projects in which people could not talk to one another on social grounds—but I suspect such circumstances are largely fantasy. A modern site crew is not structured by the class system or by any cutthroat competition to write up reports (that would be good) or by the recording system, but by the economy in which they work. Having not enough time, as in contract archaeology, and having too much, as in university archaeology, are equally damaging to precision, creativity, and productive thought. Teams react, as teams, to the challenge. Of course, there are overbearing directors and poor leaders, but they are not all made equally obnoxious by some imaginary force of social evolution.

The benefits of the reflexive approach do need to be seen in context, before this too becomes another dogma. We are suddenly being urged (e.g., by Berggren and Hodder, as by Andrews et al. 2000) to monitor our records, some 30 years after we were advised to stop doing it and dispense with our site journals, Polaroids, and video cameras—the purpose of which was exactly that—in favor of proforma recording and the Harris matrix. Happily, however, not everyone did abandon the business of recording the recording, and some of us took pains to make sure it happened by embedding it in the excavation design through recovery levels (p. 125). In my own experience of the last 38 years, whether in rescue archaeology or research, interpretation has always started at the trowel's edge, often prematurely; in fact, it was usually a challenge to get people to shut up: narrative construction went on day and night—some of it fatuous, but some truly determinant. This was, of course, because we didn't use "laborers" but volunteers, students, and professionals with degrees who had a strong interest in the outcome. When we used YOP and MSC teams, the situation was entirely different. Although paid much more than volunteers or students, they requested very clear digging instructions on an hourly basis and pleaded to be excused from writing anything at all.

Paul Everill's recent review of commercial archaeology, *The Invisible Diggers*, also raised the specter of class, this time in the United Kingdom, but it is at least based on data in the form of questionnaires filled in by employees (Everill 2009). This process itself encourages complaint, so we shouldn't be surprised if complaining is the main burden of the British profession—and, as a reviewer commented in *Antiquity*, "they are quite good at it" (Burrow 2010). Seventy-seven percent of Everill's interviewees thought the profession was in crisis and that the current system must be changed. They objected to low status and low pay, saying "site staff felt they were not treated as specialists, but often merely as laborers." They also felt that standards on site had deteriorated since the 1980s and 1990s, largely due to poor supervision and inadequate training. Some complained about the things that had attracted them in the first place—for example, the digging and being outdoors in all weathers. But the most striking result of the inquiry was that a majority of the people who were considering leaving the profession did so because they felt they were losing their love of archaeology.

Everill's recommendations were to improve training, in the universities and on the job, and to raise pay. Sure, but how? In this well-intentioned (and well-written) thesis, the profession nevertheless comes across as a beast gnawing its own wound. Its anxieties and wrongs are attributed only to those near at hand. It is a voice from deep within a trench. Let's note that every one of these complaints, all of them worthy, can be attributed to the same root cause, which has nothing to do with class, evil employers, or reflexivity. It is all about money.

## Money

It is worth repeating that in archaeology, as in the rest of the world of work, you are paid to do what is wanted by the person with the money, not to do what you would rather be doing. As in any other business, the relations of production are not caused by some inherent human nastiness, but by the job, the task in hand, and the money available. In the university sector, archaeologists are paid to research and teach and are assessed on their publications and performance. In the CRM sector, archaeologists are paid to manage the resource, record it before destruction, and to make it accessible to the public.

So there are two parallel parts to our profession: people paid to produce new research, mainly in universities, and people paid to manage research resources, mainly in government, underpinned by a large commercial sector (FIG. 3.5). Inevitably, they aim for different outcomes, because they serve different masters;

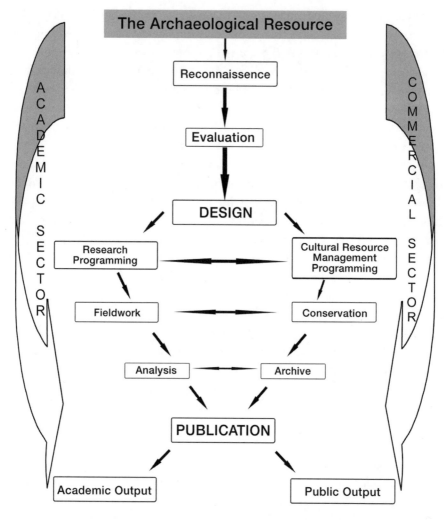

FIGURE 3.5. The double helix of professional archaeology (from Carver 2009, 360; *diagram by the author/FAS-Heritage*).

and their rules of engagement are determined by different government ministries. Could they, should they, be brought together as one discipline, one profession?

For the remainder of this chapter I am going to focus on the commercial profession, not just because that is where the complaints are, but because it is where most of the archaeological talent goes. It is a talent that is largely untapped, essentially because it is being asked to do the wrong job in the wrong way. That doesn't mean the universities are perfect—they have a problem with archaeological fieldwork too: it is often of low standard and done without recognition of their obligations to CRM. Moreover, the universities are not making enough use of the professional sector to carry out their research. But if we can reposition the work that is done in the commercial sector, and make it more satisfying to its employees, give it higher status in the eyes of our brother industries in development, and spend more on it, then much will follow. The work we do in the commercial sector will be seen as having equal kudos with that done in the university sector, and the gap between them can close.

The money in the commercial sector comes from developers who are obliged by the planning process to pay for archaeological intervention, and by their shareholders to pay as little as possible. They are not obliged to provide satisfaction and happiness for the archaeological workforce. The system they use—competitive tender—was borrowed from the USA but without the SHPOs, which would have moderated it and helped to keep up the price. Competitive tender causes everything else: low pay, insecure supervisors, lack of training time, lack of status, and, above all, loss of intellectual content.

Developers pay (or borrow the money) for a site to be cleared, foundations to be laid, and a building to be put up. The plans are put together in a design which includes some creative specialists, such as the architects, and artisans, such as the masons, and suppliers, such as those that provide the cement. These are each employed on a different basis: the architect through design competition or direct appointment, the builders and suppliers through tender. The overall price is negotiated with the aid of consultants, quality-control agents, planners, and accountants.

Where are the archaeologists in all this? In Europe, at first they were nowhere: a bunch of nomads obstinately refusing to leave the site and muttering about capitalism (I should know, I was one of them). Then regional trusts, underpinned by taxpayer support, began to negotiate their costs through the county archaeologists. Then Britain's Geoff Wainwright ushered in competitive tender via the newly created English Heritage (officially the Historic Building and Monuments Commission for England), and the price began to be driven downward. In 1990, Planning Policy Guidance Note 16 (PPG16) ensured a steady flow of evaluation work, which led mainly to the excavation of the least interesting sites (see below). Later, developers appointed their own archaeological consultants, to ensure they were not being taken for a ride.

These new kids on the block, with their fast cars and Blackberries, are assuming control of the archaeological mitigation process.

If this has resulted in a change of status, it is only marginal. Already in the 1970s, in the United States, the Society for Professional Archaeologists had attempted to raise the negotiating position of archaeologist to that of architect. We should be appointed by design competition, and we should negotiate a price appropriate to the job in hand. But this was tested in the courts and the archaeologists lost; the procurement of archaeology was no different from the procurement of gravel, and should be commissioned through competitive tender. I think it's worth following this trail where it leads, since we are talking here about the backbone of our profession and it is in no-one's interest that they should be disaffected. On one thing we can all have common cause: the standard of fieldwork must improve, its scientific repertoire must expand, and its outcome must be more imaginative. We must be more highly valued. But how?

## RAISING OUR GAME

Let's first examine how values are arrived at and then how we could profile ours to attract a more realistic level of support. As we saw earlier, traditional legislation treats our assets as "cultural property," *beni culturali*, property belonging to a state or a person which, although not yet seen, nonetheless has value. The archives of the soil are like deposits of precious metal—usually seen as coming under the prerogative of the crown. According to the UK's PPG16, deposits of *national importance* were assets equivalent to monuments, to be conserved, or their value realized by excavation where they couldn't be. Meanwhile, in the United States, these deposits were said to have *significance*, rather than importance, suggesting that their meaning was valued above their sense of property. Section 106 logic led to significant sites being worthy of investigation, while PPG16 logic meant that important sites were to be conserved, and the others (presumably unimportant) were to be investigated.

We thus have two concepts to disentangle:

- Does the value of archaeological strata lie in their being monuments or in giving knowledge?

- And if knowledge, what sort of knowledge; and what should our response be to the destruction of archaeological sites? In other words, what does mitigation really mean and how much should it cost? The malaise of our workforce, in England, implies that archaeology is undervalued by society. How could that value be raised?

Before answering that last question, we have to be sure that archaeological value has a currency that is valid worldwide. If our subject exists as a legitimate and productive human activity, then there ought to be a common human value to it; like poetry, and chemistry, the inquiry has to do with being human and sharing a planet. In science, defining commonalty is easy: the 92 elements of the periodic table are shared concepts. No community is entitled to claim there are 902, just because of its beliefs. Potassium has similar properties in Beijing, New York, Botswana, in Aboriginal Australia, and indeed on Mars. But is this true of the past? Is each community entitled to its own version of the past, not only different from that of outsiders, but morally superior?

This is the basis of the postmodern stance that has so negatively affected the archaeological project and, in particular, its scientific agenda. The most vocal supporters of this kind of extreme relativism are, paradoxically, Westerners, and many of them leading lights in the World Archaeological Congress. It is not difficult to see why this is; these scholars have worked in political situations that have convinced them that morality is more important than history. Being entitled to respect is adequate for most of us, but not always for the self-appointed champions of descendant communities who can sometimes give an unfortunate impression that these communities do not themselves understand what is at stake. Thus the subject is locked in another dogma, and once again the key that unlocks the impasse is design. Every community is used to arriving at decisions via debate—which is another way of describing the design process. In other words, giving a site its contemporary value is not a case of one argument prevailing against the others. It is the net result of reconciling different interests. For me, the resolution of value, on which the archaeological resource and a whole industry depends, is a conciliatory, not an adversarial, process.

There are three main categories of value with which planners have to wrestle when deciding what to do with a piece of land (TABLE 3.2). *Market values* include ways of creating wealth and are measured in profit, such as a shopping mall; *community values* include the creation of amenities for public benefit, or minority benefit, and are measured in votes—for example, a school or hospital; *human values* can't be measured in votes or money because they

Table 3.2. Values in the planning system

---

**MARKET VALUES**. The value is measured in terms of financial gain:

- Capital value (profit obtainable on resale)
- Production value (profit obtainable from agricultural or industrial development)
- Commercial value (profit obtainable from creating a retail outlet)
- Residential value (profit obtainable from building houses)

---

**COMMUNITY VALUES**. The value is measurable in terms of votes:

- Amenity value (provides a facility to be shared by the community)
- Political value (wins a majority of votes)
- Minority value (wins the support of an important interest group—for example, a descendant community)
- Local value (conforms to local taste)

---

**HUMAN VALUES**. These values arise from membership of the human family:

- Environmental value (protects the biosphere of wild animals and plants)
- Archaeological value (protects the sources of knowledge about the past)*

---

* "Archaeological value" is defined by matching the researach agenda, the resource model, and the social context.

mainly benefit the unborn, people who have yet to appear. But we know we want to do our best for them. Archaeological value belongs here (Carver 1996).

This does not assume that there is only one archaeological value—the Western or the scientific. It just assumes that archaeological value, as opposed to any other type, has an intellectual—not a financial, cultural, political, or sentimental—reward. Others can fight their corners for these latter. An intellectual asset can be constructed locally; it does not need to conform to a global agenda. But it may.

These ideas urge us to define the archaeological resource as a source of new knowledge. Such resources are not necessarily monuments. Some can be made into monuments, but the monument is what you have left when the knowledge has been won. Knowledge is the fruit, the monument is the peel. Thus, the redevelopment of a piece of real estate that is going to damage the archaeological deposit is an opportunity for historical research, not for rescuing a monument. Cultural resource management is not a management of political aspirations, but a management of research resources. These resources should be protected or conserved according to the opinion, obviously, of researchers. The social product of mitigation archaeology is new knowledge, not preservation by record. If accepted, these principles would transform the business of the archaeological profession and the perception of what its clients are buying.

For such a product to be successfully sold, it must be clearly described to the buyer. The idea of multivocality is an excellent one, but only if the multivocality is sought when it can have an effect on defining the outcome—that is, before a project starts. For this reason, it is not only essential to have a project design, but to publish it in advance, so as to reach all interested parties, not just the ones you'd like to hear from. Everyone should have a say on where an airplane is to fly, but once it takes off, there are limited advantages in having all the passengers in the cockpit. Consultation is followed by expertise. This is essentially the same principle as seeking planning permission. Indeed, the obligation of archaeologists to seek planning permission for their own excavations might be a useful way of seeking consensus for both research and mitigation projects. It might also raise the professional profile of the activity, with everything that follows.

## GOOD SIGNS ON THE HORIZON

So, are we making progress? I have my own suggestions to make in Chapter 6, but meanwhile I want to cite four recent initiatives that seem to me to open promising pathways—from Ireland, Sweden, the United States, and England. Forgive me if I illustrate these with quotations, but I want to persuade you that I am not relying solely on assertion or impression, but citing official statements, even if only statements of intent, that could be used in negotiation by today's fieldworkers to improve their lot and the status of archaeology in general.

The United States has had the longest experience of running a deregulated system and has the concept of a knowledge value built into its term of "significance." Let's visit ACRA, the American Cultural Resources Association, which was established in 1995 to self-regulate the multimillion-dollar CRM industry in the USA and, more importantly, to lobby other participants in the development game. It styles itself "a trade association . . . covering the fields of historic preservation, history, archaeology, architectural history, historical architecture, and landscape architecture." Its aim is "to promote professional, ethical, and business practices for the benefit of the resources, the public, and the members of the association." ACRA lists its responsibilities to the public, to its clients, to its employees, and to its colleagues. Members shall put conservation first, shall strive to respect the concerns of people whose histories and/or resources are the subject of cultural resources investigation, and shall not make exaggerated, misleading, or unwarranted statements about their work. They are "obligated to provide diligent, creative, honest, and competent services and professional advice to their clients." They undertake to exercise independent professional judgment on behalf of their clients, but at the same time they also undertake to respect their confidentiality and will accept the decisions of a client concerning the objectives and nature of the professional services, "unless the decisions involve conduct that is illegal or inconsistent with the ACRA member's obligations to the public interest." This might seem like quite a balancing act, given that the client is a developer and primarily interested in building a new road or putting up a new building, rather than adding a few footnotes to history. But a declared list of mutually supportive obligations of this kind makes it easier to win respect from cooperating professions and harder for clients to get work done on the cheap. The assumption here is that archaeological knowledge from research is the product paid for by a developer. Thus, while competitive tender still applies, the status of an ACRA company allows some latitude for negotiated costs, with quality control delivered by the SHPO (*http://acra-crm.org/*).

To try to enlarge their research dividend from rescue projects, Irish archaeologists got together in 2006 to address the schism in Irish archaeology, as they saw it, between university and commercial archaeology, with a collaborative policy document called *2020*—subtitled "Repositioning Irish Archaeology in the Knowledge Society." They sketched the brave new world for the 21st-century profession assuming a massive number of archaeologists working in the commercial sector (at least in times of boom). They noted that government had currently failed to keep up with this new constituency, having no coherent structure or policy for it; they regretted the disconnectedness between development-led archaeology and research, the failure to create and publish new knowledge from this massive investment, and to provide for archiving and storage.

They asked for three "overarching enabling measures" to be put into effect without delay:

- An archaeological implementation partnership—a kind of public/private committee that would decide on what was to happen on big projects
- A Bureau for Archaeological Publication to tackle the backlog, create archives, and underwrite publications

■ And an inter-institutional collaborative research funding system, drawing attention to the fact that, almost alone in Europe, Ireland and Britain had virtually no collaborative procedure between the universities and the consultancy sector. They suggested priming cooperation by setting up a fund of €5 million per annum to work on big projects (University College Dublin 2006).

Insofar as any of this has happened, it had not noticeably closed the gap between the universities and the consultants by the time of the 2008 banking crisis, which affected both. But if we are allowed another clear run at the future, some mechanism to encourage these two sectors to work together is essential. It may not be best done through government or a QUANGO (quasi-autonomous non-governmental organization)—that just creates a proxy state archaeological service with no funding. As urged here, it is better to look at how procurement could itself be modified, to give research and knowledge creation greater prominence in the mission.

Sweden attempted to build research into the procurement process by amending its laws. In its Proposition 1993/94:177, the Swedish government decided that CRM mitigation was in need of a more visible research dividend, and that every project commissioned by a developer should be part of a "progressive research process." Collaboration between the universities and commercial companies would be closer, and the companies should feel themselves part of the national research network (see Carver 2001).

In 2006, another Swedish government paper looked toward the heritage management of the future (Swedish National Heritage Board 2006). In this vision, heritage management should enable the landscape to tell stories, and the authors asked for the humanistic and historical aspects of the historic environment to be strengthened and internationalized. The paper warned that the increase of archaeological actors in the marketplace would lead to the commercialization of archaeology and affect how it is rated by the public. It wanted better links between the research and practical parts of the profession—that is, the universities and the commercial and government sectors. It urged a more open, more international, and more "aggressive" approach to heritage management. These statements are always rather oracular—it gives them longer life, I suppose; but here I have lined up the three main recommendations, quoted verbatim, with what I think they imply:

- Increased readiness to manage landscapes in transition (= more access)

- Strengthening humanistic and historical perspectives (= more research)

- Formulate modern assignments (= more private initiatives).

Taken together, this would mean a loosening up of the government grip in favor of a more frontline role for heritage in the economy.

But it is actually in the United Kingdom where we can welcome, with modest excitement, a new awareness of who needs archaeology and why it should be paid for. Curiously, although one of these initiatives (PPS5) is from government, another, which preceded it, came out of the building industry itself, and we'll visit that first.

CEEQUAL, which appeared in 2008, is the Civil Engineering Quality Assessment and Awards Scheme, initiated by the Institute of Civil Engineers and managed by a private company. Engineering companies submit projects which are assessed by CEEQUAL on their economic, environmental, and *social* success. Projects are scored 10 to 0 under a long list of headings, and winners get awards. Success indicates an ability to push through a sustainable development in conformity with government policy. This clearly helps win new contracts and thus appeals to self-interest. Section 5, one of the longest, deals with the Historic Environment. Evidence to be cited in 5.3.3 to 5.3.5 (with 8 points each) should establish how a project has positively protected any historic environment assets, how good design has enhanced and valued the historic environment, how any innovative methods or collaborations have enabled the conservation of historic environment assets, and how any archaeological investigation or building recording has contributed to local and national research agendas. Other sections deal with post-excavation, liaison with local societies, and public access to the site (CEEQUAL 2008). This document, prepared by the engineering profession, is thus more persuaded of archaeology's value as a generator of new knowledge than most governments or even the archaeology profession itself. All that is needed to upgrade the archaeologist's seat at the table is an agreement by the government that this is what we do.

So, finally, to the new PPS5 (Planning Policy Statement) for England issued in 2010—do we see any sign here of a change in the official view? Indeed we do. PPS5 defines archaeological resources like this: "Those parts of the historic environment that have significance because of their historic, archaeological, architectural or artistic interest are called heritage assets. Some heritage assets possess a level of interest that justifies designation." "Archaeological value" is here replaced by "archaeological interest," defined as "an interest in carrying out an expert investigation at some point in the future into the evidence a heritage asset may hold of past human activity." In other words, archaeological assets are being treated not as a monument but as a research resource. So far so good. Furthermore, among the government's objectives in planning for the historic environment are "to contribute to our knowledge and understanding of our past by ensuring that opportunities are taken to capture evidence from the historic environment and to make this publicly available, particularly where a heritage asset is to be lost." This is a massive improvement on PPG16. Other aspects to be welcomed are that developers must put the evaluation in the public domain, and are required to publish any mitigating excavations they fund. The broader and more research-heavy "significance" has replaced "importance."

But the basic response to a threatened site is still the same: a planning application requires an archaeological evaluation based on desktop assessment and field evaluation where necessary. And the balance is still in favor of preservation: "A documentary record of our past is not as valuable as retaining the heritage asset, and therefore the ability to record evidence of our past should not be a factor in deciding whether a proposal that would result in a heritage asset's destruction should be given consent" (Department for Communities and Local Government 2010). A documentary record is, of course, much less than an archaeological research project; and PPS5 stops short of implying that excavation for research purposes increases the significance not only of that asset, but of all the adjacent sites.

One reason for this is no doubt a fear that development would cease because research of one site would raise the significance of all its neighbors, inviting their protection. But another reason is both more simple and less rational: research is still the business of another ministry. The heritage in England is in a separate ministry from research, thus emphasizing its genesis as a non-intellectual concept. It comes under Culture, Media and Sport, and its planning comes under the Department of Communities and Local Government. However, research is infiltrating into the fabric of these institutions here and there. Paragraph 134 of the Historic Environment Planning Practice Guide itemizes the *Content of Written Scheme of Investigation* in 13 paragraphs—very close to the spirit and matter of a project design, including publication (English Heritage 2010). For projects that are to be paid for by English Heritage itself, much more detailed guidance is given by *Management of Research Projects in the Historic Environment*, or MoRPHE, both for the content of a project design and for the cycle for the project's management. MoRPHE replaces the more reactive MAP2 (p. 140), and flies the research flag not only in its title, but in its list of good practices, the first of which is "the creation of knowledge" (English Heritage 2008). Under MoRPHE, Project Design is led by a Project Proposal—so that a company has a chance to bid for work without incurring large costs. By the same token, if the project is accepted, its proponent can be paid to develop the project design. This is an excellent idea. Obviously, the intention is that archaeological projects funded by developers should follow a similar ethos and procedure.

Thus, in spite of the paradox that CRM archaeology is in the wrong ministry, English Heritage has succeeded in moving a long way toward the idea that the past exists as something to be known, rather than simply kept, and would seem to support the concept of archaeology as a fundamental human value, more than a community or market value.

## Is the Argument Won?

We will have to wait a bit to see what kind of impact PPS5 has—but I fear it will only have an impact in England. It does not tackle the question of competitive tender or price, so in some ways it is asking for a research frill to be pasted onto a proposal, rather than for research objectives to force the pace and determine the degree of intervention and the price. It does not tackle the question of quality control, which is crucial at a time of declining standards; neither the public nor the developers nor the media has a mechanism for distinguishing a good excavation from a bad one.

As a final pointer to the direction in which archaeological procurement should be heading, we can look at the manifesto published as *The Government's Statement on the Historic Environment for England* (HM Government 2010). Adopting the rubric "historic environment" doesn't sound too optimistic, since an environment is some sort of static wrap, something you want to keep for various reasons: nostalgic or sentimental (it's good for votes), or economic (it's good for tourism). But it turns out that the British government at least gives a strong steer toward the idea that "historic environment" *only* has a meaning if it is powered by archaeological research. That's why it supports the direction of funds toward research projects that "explore our past." It emphasizes this position by highlighting policies that have actually been implemented, and by encouraging other agencies to help in the business:

- The Heritage Lottery Fund has been able to support over 30,000 projects at a cost of £4.3 billion.

- The Aggregates Levy Sustainability Fund has provided around £30 million, including a significant contribution to archaeological research.

- As a major funder of archaeology, the commercial development sector has also contributed to important research.

The government also recognizes the historic environment as a wealth creator—in that people at home and abroad take it as a reason why they travel. For many, heritage has become an increasingly popular leisure time activity, and around 70% of all adults make an active choice to visit historic places every year. In other words, like PPS5, it takes conservation as a given, but realizes that without access there can be no inclusivity. And without curiosity, there is nothing to inspire access. And research is just curiosity on its best behavior.

## CONCLUSION

I make no apology for inflicting these documents on you; they are—especially the English Heritage studies—world leaders and of global relevance, the fruits of the struggle to make archaeology both productive and accessible in a climate of diminishing expenditure by central government and increasing domination by the market. It seems likely that if countries are not yet affected by this phenomenon, they will be shortly.

However, all this talk of research makes the glaring omission more glaring still: what has happened to the universities? This elephant is not in the room or apparently on the same island. We shall have to return to this problem—and Chapter 5 will provide us with an opportunity. For the moment, we can note that the reason is no doubt the same as always: these papers are issued by DCMS (Culture, Media and Sport), and universities are governed by the DES (Education and Science). Yet DCMS does do research, and DES does do ethics. Could we conceive of a policy on the environment, on engineering, or on geological exploration without a mention of the universities? Of course not, so why is it just us? Research, at least the way that real field archaeologists do it, is itself the basis for the interest in the past that powers the historic environment. And research is what universities do.

If archaeological research can be thought of, as English Heritage and the British government apparently now do, as giving added value to a development project as a whole, then the archaeologist comes in as a creative agent, like the architect, rather than as a supplier of services. In this case, archaeologists can be chosen on the basis of the new past they can create, not on the basis of how cheap and pliable they are; and everything else follows: higher price, higher kudos, greater job satisfaction, and, indeed, a better career structure.

This is not just desirable but essential. In Chapter 2, I tried to persuade you that we are, in general, performing field archaeology at many levels below its potential capacity and competence. In this chapter, I argue that while archaeologists respect the social context in which they work, it is not clear that society gives reciprocal respect to the archaeology they do. It would be good to propose a structure in which those working in archaeology are elevated to a higher professional level by being seen as part of the design team. Is that possible? We first need to test its feasibility by taking a look at what different countries do and ask why they do it. That should show us whether it is the objectives, the terrain, or the social context that is most instrumental in constructing fieldwork, whether design is really determinant. Besides, this has been all rather abstract, and we need to get out into the fresh air. I propose a quick world tour, where we will meet different field archaeologists and see how they rose to the challenges confronting them.

# CHAPTER 4

# DESIGN ON TOUR

## INTRODUCTION

I f doing archaeology were an empirical exercise, intended to collect data or to preserve it by record, we would expect it to adopt standard methods of intervention and recording that could be applied everywhere, resulting in procedures that were economic, effective, and consistent. But if it were an investigation, intended to maximize knowledge from each opportunity, then we would expect its practitioners to approach every situation differently, adapting a large and flexible toolbox to the opportunity in question. In this case, the variations in approach would not be matters of teaching or doctrine, but attempts to reconcile the particular variables encountered. In my contention, the principal variables are the objectives, the terrain, and the social context in which we work.

To demonstrate that the second of these two procedures—namely, archaeology as investigation—is both the more appropriate and the more widely practiced, I have pulled together a small bundle of projects, some recent, some less recent, selected from different parts of the world. The aim is to show how each challenge has been met, with ingenuity, adaptation, and invention—in other words, although the archaeologists in question seldom say so, by design.

One can make a case for each of the three main variables as being preeminent in decision-making. *Objectives* have the broadest range and ought to be the determinant driver of projects. *Terrain* too will determine the responses of those who seek to examine it; so inasmuch as this chapter has a structure, I have organized it by different kinds of site and ambience. But my conclusion, perhaps surprisingly, is that the *social context* is often most influential in determining how archaeology is done, particularly where practice is standardized.

## IN THE DESERT

Let's go first to Arizona in the company of one of my heroes, Alfred Kidder. In the 1920s he was working in *terra incognita*, guided only by the place-names given by the Spanish to the settlements they had found on arrival. Kidder selected one of these—Pecos—and excavated a trench through it, to give him a pottery sequence from the earliest occupation to the latest. Using this pottery, he then conducted surveys over the wider territory, not digging, but using surface finds to put into dated order the settlements they implied. The result was the story of the Ancestral Puebloan people: where they settled, when they flourished, how their territory contracted, and the fact of their mysterious decline before the arrival of conquerors from the east (Kidder 1924).

One natural successor to this inquiry was the survey of the Virú Valley in Peru, designed by Julian Steward, William Strong, Wendell Bennett, and Gordon Willey in 1946, which delivered another fieldwork classic. The archaeological aim of the project was to discover the date and distribution of the prehistoric settlements, which were held to "reflect the natural environment, the level of technology on which the builders operated, and various institutions of social interaction and control which the culture maintained." Again, excavators established a pottery typology and cultural sequence, which were then deployed in a surface survey that was to record more than 300 sites covering 5,000 years. Each site was numbered (V-1, V-2, etc.), visited, planned with compass and chain, and a pottery sample taken from the surface. About half the sites showed no noteworthy features above ground, but where they did, the exposed walls of stones or adobe were measured and their masonry described. Test pits were sometimes dug to measure the depth of deposit. The pottery populations, both from the surface and the stratified sequences, were placed in an order—or "seriated"—according to the percentages of the different types present. The result was a historical geography of settlement and the dynamics of its development (Willey 1953).

All parties were aware of the problem of creating such a narrative on the basis of such partial recovery: "The greatest single weakness in the present study is the associational dating," wrote Willey. Many sites had different kinds (and periods) of ceramics on the surface, but it was unclear which ceramic period referred to visible structures. In other sites, particularly in the lowland areas, sites appeared to represent a single period from the surface collections, but earlier periods lay hidden beneath. The report, published in 1953 and revisited in 1999, was blessed with an unusually detailed and self-critical account of the methodology and was notable for its sensitivity to the modern landscape and its inhabitants. It could be said that, for all its own misgivings, here was a project that had successfully matched its objectives, terrain, and modern social context.

This exploratory approach has had a long legacy. In 1999 Frank Eddy and Fred Wendorf published their neat Sinai survey, undertaken in a modern framework of resource management. They had heard about the proposed reclamation of desert for agriculture in the upper Wadi Girafi Basin, where the Egyptian government planned to relocate 2 million farmers. After an initial reconnaissance in 1994, they put a formal survey on the ground in 1996, locating 72 potential sites. Three teams performed an intensive full-coverage survey with on-site recording of ruins and artifacts (without pick-up). As a result, they could propose ten types of site and they selected a representative ten examples from them for excavation. The results led them to conclude that the land had been occupied just once before—by pastoralists of the copper age. Thus a large desert landscape had been provided both with a narrative and enhanced heritage value.

Survey in open, arid terrain naturally depends on the visibility of ruins and artifacts on the surface. But we are often dealing with structures that are ephemeral in the extreme, easily scattered by wind, scavengers, or bad-tempered camels. Clues come from photographs taken in the 19th century, such as Geronimo's wickiup, made of branches and cloth, and rediscoverable only as open spaces ringed by cleared rocks (Seymour 2009). In southern Montana, Laura Scheiber and Judson Finley (2010) set out to map and save elusive traces like these and have them accepted as heritage assets (FIG. 4.1). In this approach, the stone rings are mapped in detail by hand and located by GPS; their hearths are located by fluxgate survey and sampled for radiocarbon dating, and the results displayed in layered maps using GIS. Different social groups had different floor plans, so, even where artifacts are missing, the movement of particular peoples can be dated and mapped. The results also established a heritage value for this, the dominant type of "monument" in the Bighorn Canyon National Recreational Area.

In Australia, Patricia Fanning and her colleagues have also designed ways of defining the elusive imprint of early peoples in arid country (Fanning et al. 2009). Hearths are a principal indicator of aboriginal activity and a key property for heritage managers. But they survive in a wide range of conditions, classified in six grades: A = buried; B = partially exposed; C = intact; D = disturbed; E = scattered; and F = remnant. There is effectively no stratification of the occupation. Events take place on the surface or at the interface

91

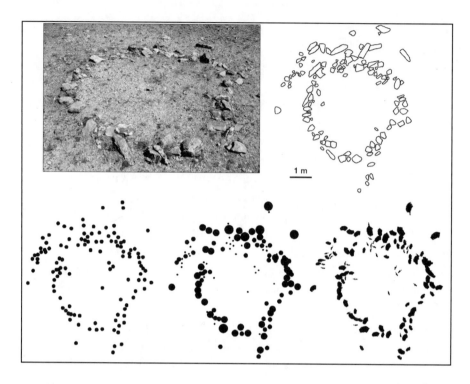

FIGURE 4.1. Desert imprints: a stone circle (tipi ring) in the northwest American plains, showing photograph, plan, and three diagrams representing the stones by size: no size (*left*), graduated by size (*center*), and representing size and orientation of each stone (*right*) (from Scheiber and Finlay 2010, fig. 7; *courtesy of Laura Scheiber and* Antiquity).

between two sedimentary episodes. A fluxgate magnetometer shows which scatters really were hearths (p. 52), and the sedimentary sequence above and below the hearths can be dated by OSL and C14 (Rhodes et al. 2009). In these huge areas of intermittent use, without obvious pattern, an "archaeological surface" is defined as any land surface that has stone artifacts and hearths, using indicators that can be detected, assessed, and mapped without digging. Such low-impact approaches are popular with aborigines, the traditional owners (or TOs), because the sites can be characterized without disturbing them. Similar methods could perhaps be applied to the Mesolithic in temperate Europe, another type of ephemeral site that provides a headache for heritage managers, although there the remains are often buried and even less visible.

## INSIDE CAVES

Caves famously provide long-term strata traps out of reach of flood and deflation, preserving a better record of even the most elusive desert folk. Many caves are just rock shelters, some unvisited for millennia and never rained on, and the deposit is as dry as flour and can be just as inscrutable. Dust Cave in Alabama, attractively described by its researchers as a "karstic vestibule," had 4 vertical meters of strata. Sarah Sherwood and her team began with five test pits, then three test excavations, then seven test units to bedrock, and then an area 2 × 12 m examined in 1 m squares dug in spits each 1 cm deep (Sherwood et al. 2004). Since layers (i.e., contexts) are often hard to define in caves with any clarity, the researchers divided the deposit by means of "lithostratigraphy." Groups, subgroups, and tertiary lenses provided the basic structure, with hearths and finds marking episodes of occupation. These were dated with 43 radiocarbon dates to give a sequence beginning in 11,000 cal BC. In this way, the excavators learned to distinguish alluvium, rock fall, underground riverbeds (phreatic aquifers), erosion, animal burrows, and "prepared clay surfaces," that is, clay layers about 1 m across and 1–3 cm thick, typically burnt with a thin layer of ash. These were the dramatis personae of the cave sequence.

What's not to like about Dust Cave? Carefully evaluated. Clear design. Use of an appropriate system of detecting and recording sequence. British readers might wonder about the test pits, but ethically they are helpful: the deposit has not been totally excavated, leaving strata for future questions we don't yet know how to ask. The cave entrance is now protected against looters with a gate.

Clearly the challenge that remains is to improve the reading of these sequences, which cover such long representative periods of deep time and are composed of a million strata which are so hard to see. At Dust Cave, Sarah Sherwood and her colleagues could distinguish some stratigraphic landmarks in the form of clay surfaces and learned to distinguish water action and wind blow. Similarly at Troubat, Natalie Fourment (2004) used a method that seems to work well in France—the orientation of flint objects. Broadly, where the artifacts lie randomly in all directions, they probably indicate an occupation surface; where they align, they are more likely the result of a stream washing through the cave. Another approach uses geophysical scanning, as Andy Herries did at Pinnacle Point (p. 52). Ben Keys and Lynley Wallis at Gledswood Cave in NW Queensland noted that magnetic susceptibility readings varied with depth and thus time. They noted a high correlation between mag sus values and artifact distributions and used it to indicate human occupation in situ. They also deployed several other proxies to inform their sequence: loss on ignition showed organic content, as did phosphorus; particle-size analysis distinguished water flow from wind blow (Keys 2009).

Thus, although sequence is important to cave excavators, there are two caveats: (1) Contexts are hard to define and harder still to sequence; excavators have been obliged to advance a long way beyond the idea that visible stratification is all you need. (2) Ethical constraints do not encourage the investigation of cave life in area excavations; whatever level was chosen—assuming it could be located in plan—would require the destruction of everything above it.

By contrast, let's visit a cave where human activity was more widely spread over a larger area. Between them, Mammoth Cave and Salts Cave in Kentucky are large enough: they extend for 145 miles underground, so far (FIG. 4.2a, b;

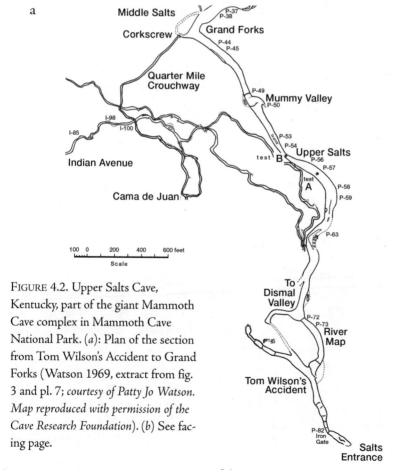

FIGURE 4.2. Upper Salts Cave, Kentucky, part of the giant Mammoth Cave complex in Mammoth Cave National Park. (*a*): Plan of the section from Tom Wilson's Accident to Grand Forks (Watson 1969, extract from fig. 3 and pl. 7; *courtesy of Patty Jo Watson. Map reproduced with permission of the Cave Research Foundation*). (*b*) See facing page.

Watson 1969; 1997). Not all of this vast area was occupied in prehistoric times—in fact, apparently, very little of it was. The caves were used to extract salts (gypsum, mirabilite, epsomite: i.e., calcium, sodium, and magnesium sulfate), which were used for decoration and as purgatives. The miners were Woodland people of the last two millennia BC, and they left animal remains, plants, faeces, textiles, baskets, and tools, and most abundantly, prehistoric

FIGURE 4.2. (*cont.*) (*b*): Mummy Valley (Watson 1969, extract from fig. 3 and pl. 7; *courtesy of Patty Jo Watson. Photo by James Dyer and William T. Austin reproduced with permission of the Cave Research Foundation and of the Illinois State Museum*).

torches and hearths (probably for guidance too). Occasionally they left themselves as mummified corpses.

Of course, the first systematic explorers did not know this. As a student, the now eminent archaeologist Patty Jo Watson met her husband Richard who was a caver, and they set out to make sense of Mammoth and Salts with a newly formed archaeological cave team. They began by dividing the main passage known as "Wilson's Accident to Mummy Valley" into 50 m lengths and subdividing it into 10 m lengths. In the first phase of exploration, they quickly found that it was "virtually impossible to define all of the features (in particular the nature and degree of mining activity, and the extent and intensity of smoke blackening) in a way that enabled them to be meaningfully quantified." In 1969, they described their strategy as (1) reconnaissance observation and collection of some 70 representative items; and (2) excavation of two small test areas in Upper Salts. This acted as a first evaluation of the strata in this vast mine. It wasn't so much a site as a highway punctuated by occasional scorching from flares, mineral seams, and, of course, accidents: "Lost John," a 45-year-old male, 5 feet 3 inches tall, was found in 1935 mummified by the dry air. He was partially crushed under the fallen boulder that had knocked him out and broken his arm. He had also been eaten by rats (or "damaged by rodent activity," as we archaeologists say).

In this huge system, reconnaissance and evaluation have naturally continued for more than 40 years, and there has been a good appreciation that excavation will not say much without it. Meanwhile, new technology for underground mapping has replaced the old tapes and torches, and new questions can be answered by smaller, better-targeted excavations.

## COLD AS ICE

From hot and dry to cold and wet: Vladimir Pitulko has been working out how to access prehistoric peoples now walled up in permafrost (2007; 2008). Previously the part of Siberia he researches had been visited with notably robust inquiries. In the 19th and early 20th centuries, the frozen tombs were attacked with dynamite and the bodies and grave goods freed with copious amounts of boiling water. The cemetery of mammoths at Berelekh, Yakutia, was excavated using a high-pressure water-jet. "The effect of such a practice at any archaeological site is disastrous," comments Pitulko; "Thawing must be natural. Of the normal methods of engineers, fires upset radiocarbon dating; steam damages objects and explosions are liable to make craters." Well observed. Pitulko prefers a gentle stream of warm air, as in the case of the Taimyr mammoth, cut out as a block in early spring and flown by helicopter to Zharkov, where it was excavated with the aid of hairdryers.

In the reconnaissance stage, sites in the permafrost are located by back-tracking from Palaeolithic debris found in melt-water outlets. Geophysics can't reach that deep, radar attenuates in the high conductivity, and locating strata using test pits (7–8 m through permanent ice) would be something of a challenge. There is a highly destructive and confusing system of ice wedges that melt and reform—and the reformed ice wedges (RIWs) can measure 5 ×5 m in plan and 20 m in depth (FIG. 4.3a).

Permafrost sites divide into three: those surface sites that melt seasonally, those that don't, and those that lie beneath the permanent ice. The first kind is contained within the seasonal thawing layer or STL. You wait for it to thaw and then dig normally. The second type, as excavated at Zhokhov, lies just beneath the STL, which is stripped off, and the exposed frozen surface is gridded as normal and divided into three areas. The first of these is opened and lies awaiting the thaw; the next has thawed and is being pumped dry; and the third is being excavated. Normal troweling and sieving are used, but photography is limited to clean surfaces at midday to avoid reflection of flash off the ice (Pitulko 2007).

The third type of site remains deep-frozen, and unlike the majority of Palaeolithic sites, which were destroyed in the post-Pleistocene thaw, this type still lies buried under 10–20 m of refrozen mineral ballast. They can only be accessed from riverbanks and dug out sideways (FIG. 4.3b). As with an example investigated at Yana, this kind of excavation is exceedingly dangerous, since it relies on strata exposed by the collapse of the 20 m high riverbank as it thaws: "The process results in abundant mud flows carrying blocks of turf, shrubs and trees." The spoil is hosed into the river using pressure hoses, and the strata and objects are recorded as the debris rushes past you. "The excavator's personal qualities," says Pitulko, "must include a great deal of patience and ingenuity"—not to mention raw courage (2008).

## INSIDE TOMBS

Working in a deep freeze has its advantages. In the frozen tombs of Siberia, the preservation is stunning, and burial with grave goods continued there into the 18th century, when Christianity began to arrive. The location of the later tombs is well known, and documents sometimes indicate who lies within them. Preservation is relative: the East Siberian temperatures vary from −50 °C in

FIGURE 4.3. Excavating in permafrost, Siberia. (*a*): Excavation of a Type 2 site at Zhokhov below the STL (seasonally thawing layer). Note the RIW (reformed ice wedge) (Pitulko 2007, fig. 2; *courtesy of Vladimir Pitulko*). (*b*): Excavation of a Type 3 site at Yana beneath 20 m of permafrost. The arrows show the direction of collapse on thawing (Pitulko 2008, fig. 4; *courtesy of Vladimir Pitulko*).

winter to +30 °C in summer. Water enters the pit of the frozen tombs in the summer, freezes in the winter, and doesn't really thaw out thereafter. Bodies in tree-trunk coffins remain protected from the thaw in supercooled air, unless entered by the tunnels of robbers—which themselves bring in more water which then freezes to ice. So the bodies survive in four states of preservation: deep frozen, dried, partially decomposed and damp, and skeletal.

Eric Crubézy and his colleagues, who are using the tombs to study ideological change, show something of the sophistication (Crubézy et al. 2009). The "Arbre Chamanique 1" or "Shaman's Tree no. 1," for example, was a tomb containing five bodies: a young man, a young woman, an old woman, and two children variously conserved in a tree-trunk coffin. Where the remains were frail, autopsies were done on the spot—but the young woman (with well-preserved organs) was taken to the lab. Grave goods included saddles, shoes, boots, and pots, and the people were magnificently dressed. Key cultural markers included the "Mongolian" haircut recognizable in preserved, dressed hair.

What did the burial rite mean? In prehistoric times we are ready—perhaps too ready—to assume a principal subject (the man) and subsidiary offerings of things and people. But, in this case, the matter could be resolved with DNA, because this too was conserved in the frozen conditions. DNA taken from the body tissue showed that the old woman was the immediate mitochondrial ancestor of the young woman and the two children. A grandchild was also identified, buried in an adjacent tomb a few meters away. Similarly, the Shaman's Tree man was the ancestor of a modern Y-chromosome group comprising 50% of the modern population tracing its origin to a 15th-century ancestor. The people in the tomb were members of the same family. As the author points out, here was a case in which DNA was not a side interest or an add-on but determinant for the interpretation. Research questions about Christian conversion were replaced by research questions on consanguinity, thanks to the exceptional state of preservation; and this in turn was owed to the terrain.

Going a little farther south, to Korea, we find another example of amazing preservation—in this case, owed to the method of burial (Eun-Joo Lee et al. 2009). In the Korean Middle Ages, high-ranking persons were buried fully clothed within two nested coffins placed in a pit that was backfilled with a lime and soil mixture that later turned into concrete. In Eung Tae's burial, the corpse had a number of letters of farewell attached to it—from a brother, the father, and most movingly from his wife, who wrote clearly under great stress, asking why he had deserted her and their son. As tradition urged, she had also woven him a pair of shoes out of her own hair, with a note to that effect; and there was a lock of hair with another note from his wife saying, "Do not discard this; bury it beside him." It was the letters that allowed Eung Tae to be identified from the Clan Lineage Book and his date of death as 1586.

But in spite of such heart-rending personal and historical detail, the excavators were obliged to return the body for reburial without analysis, so we know little more about his health and physiognomy than the letters tell us. This is in apparent accordance with the ethical position urged by the World Archaeological Congress on the respect given to human remains, and widely adopted. But here the dead are being accorded much greater respect than the living. If Eung Tae had died today, the police would not hesitate to take DNA samples of his whole family and all the suspects. On this occasion, design could perhaps have married ethics better with science: if the successor community agreed—and why wouldn't they, in one of the world's leading scientific nations?—reburial could easily follow a low-impact examination in a laboratory, so that everyone wins.

## HOT, WET, AND LEAFY

Now the scene changes to jungle and strata interlaced with roots, beetles, and burrowing mammals—strata that remain almost alive. In the Pacific Ocean, agriculture and indeed settlement are well documented as diffusionary processes spreading from Southeast Asia clockwise round the ocean. Taro, yam, banana, sweet potato, pig, and chicken were transported by canoe starting from ca. 3000 BC, and eventually arriving in New Zealand around AD 1314. However, "agriculture" does not have to arrive at the same time as the first humans, and it has its own subsequent phases of development, reflecting local social strategies. Agricultural markers in this terrain include canals, terracing, plant remains, and soil structures. On Hawai'i, Mark McCoy and Michael Graves have disentangled the sequences of agricultural terraces from their folk history using aerial survey, ground survey, auger samples, and test pits (McCoy and Graves 2010; Vitousek et al. 2004). The terrain is well zoned today, with dry soils and watered soils hard up against each other. Agriculture was aimed first at "sweet spots" with moderate rainfall and good soils. But toward the end of the prehistoric period (after AD 1400), search for new fields meant irrigation, by cutting canals and building terraces; these can be sampled and dated with C14. The dry areas don't have terraces, but windbreak field systems with low banks (like speed bumps) defining fields and preventing the erosion of those light dusty soils (which the sweet potato likes). Observing the dated sequence, the researchers worked out that the earliest settlement in the Kohala district, AD 1200–1400 (C14), subsequently expanded across the eastern dry gulches, first using windbreaks and then terraces. This achieved a surplus and gave rise to hierarchies, chiefdoms, and so to feudal land tenure. This in turn prompted more expansion to serve new lords.

Finding out directly what was being grown is not easy. Soils are notoriously mixed and subject to disturbance and ingestion by organisms macro, micro, and nano. At Kuk, Tim Denham and colleagues found that doing X-rays of soil blocks was more informative than micromorphology—the X-rays showed roots and voids and some microstratigraphy (2009). Taro, yams, and bananas were identified from phytoliths, and weeds from diatoms. Interpretation becomes clearer once you realize that, in general, the microassemblages extracted from layers or from pits represent secondary or tertiary displacements from layers lower down. These can sometimes be pinpointed from their residual pollen and spores. Combining all methods together allows an estimate to be made of what was happening when—another way of reading opaque stratification.

In thick jungle, one might expect soil to have been worked into a completely homogeneous mush by organisms large and small, since, stratigraphically, a jungle is not unlike a big garden. Lindsay Lloyd-Smith's investigations in metal-age Borneo give cause for more optimism (pers. comm.). Bone preservation is poor, but metal is present and so are some strata. Metal-age settlers move every five years or so, dismantling their houses, which were probably constructed on stilts, as today. The strata survive as layers formed of natural leaf mold and stuff fallen through raised floors—including bits of clay hearths and hearth stones (FIG. 4.4). The posts leave post-holes, and these can be picked

FIGURE 4.4. Test pit beneath a house on stilts in tropical Sarawak, Borneo (*photo by Graeme Barker; courtesy of Lindsay Lloyd Smith*).

up with mag sus and resistivity. Old occupation areas sometimes show up as chance finds of fruit trees generated by discarded pips, following which an area may be surveyed using geophysics and ground-truthed using test pits. For every terrain, there is a particular basket of investigative methods.

## EASTERN ASIA

Let's stay in East Asia for a bit longer and pay a quick visit to China and Vietnam to get a taste of what digging looks like there. In China, archaeology has a Ministry of Cultural Relics with regional offices, and universities generally team up with the ministry for both research and rescue. But Chinese friends say that only *some* universities are considered eligible to form these partnerships. Nevertheless, this shows the advantage of a regulated regime—the profession and the academy working together—at least in theory.

Rescue and research sites make extensive use of the "box" method of excavation, but it is interesting to note that this is not thought to owe anything to Mortimer Wheeler (p. 19). The method is credited to T. C. Passek in 1930s Russia, whence it came to China at an important moment of Russian influence (Liangren 2011). In the 1950s, Russian approaches and methods were deliberately sought, Chinese archaeologists being inspired by the new Marxist socioeconomic agenda to recover settlements on a large scale, but used the $2 \times 2$ m box as the essential element of control. This method, entitled "small excavation unit with large-scale exposure," was then fruitfully applied to rescue sites as development took off (Liangren 2011) (FIG. 4.5; China, State Administration of Cultural Heritage 2007, 38). Although the new agenda was meant to woo archaeologists away from the unearthing of rich monuments of the elite, the study of tombs naturally had to continue. Ironically, it was the construction of fallout shelters during the later Sino-Soviet confrontation that led to some of the most dramatic tomb excavations. This is a field in which Chinese archaeologists have reached levels of consummate skill (China, State Administration of Cultural Heritage 2007, 38; Carver 2009, 173–174).

There is plenty of clay in Southeast Asia, in some ways a nightmare material to dig in—it bakes hard as a brick in summer and goes into a slimy slurry in winter. In the clays round the Red River Valley in North Vietnam, archaeologists do big area excavations and work with special trowels that can pick as well as scrape (FIG. 4.6). Vietnam is making a major investment in heritage. Its approach to digging owes something to the French or to Europe, and involves

FIGURE 4.5. Excavations in China, 2006. Neolithic settlement at Laopodi, Guizhou, using the box method (from China 2007, 35).

FIGURE 4.6. Excavating the stiff stony clay, in area, using a purpose-built trowel in Hanoi, Vietnam (*photo by the author*).

big area excavations designed to furnish the country with a range of monuments that are its own—not necessarily under the direct influence of China. This is the homeland of the Dong Son drum, which we met in Cambodia (p. 62). However, it seems likely that the strongest influences on archaeological practice in the next decade will be coming from China, so we should not be surprised to see the emergence of the box method in Southeast Asia. Its advantages are obvious, both from the viewpoint of terrain—strata hard to see—and the social context—large sites, large workforces, big questions, and the need for detailed control.

If the box system is popular in China, the test pit (otherwise "analytical unit") is very widespread, and its natural home lies in the Americas (Black and Jolly 2003, 16; King 2005, 70–73; see also here, p. 116). We have noted the convenience of their application to the solution of problems in terrain that is difficult of access or sensitive to intrusion. Test pits (as the name implies) are often used in the evaluation stage, where they test the depth and character of the strata. But in some cases they also provide the principal instruments in the implementation of a research design. Michael Schiffer's trend-setting Joint Site (1976) showed how the rooms of a standing pueblo and the area around it could be explored with an array of randomly distributed test pits and trenches. Normand Hammond's Cuello site was approached in a similar way (Hammond 1991b). Leaving aside the rationale drawn from social theory (p. 22), we can note that test pits also allow greater control to excavation directors, especially where the strata are elusive or complex and hard to manage; and they equally provide a good way to train and exercise a dedicated voluntary workforce.

## FLAT EUROPE

I now take us back to Europe, in order to show that here too, where we are often ready to congratulate ourselves on the merits of a standard approach, we also field a wide diversity of methods—and have good reasons for it. Test pits are used for evaluation but are not thought to be a valid way of answering research questions or of thoroughly retrieving the information from a site before its destruction. By contrast, open-area excavation is certainly one of the most common responses in temperate countries both in town and country. Why is this?

Throughout Europe, numerous settlements and cemeteries are situated on Pleistocene sands and gravels—now usually taking the form of river terraces.

These terraces were convenient in prehistory and are convenient today—not only do we endlessly cut roads across them, but we like to quarry them to extract gravel and sand to build the roads. Archaeologists have some useful defensive weapons, in that the soils are often shallow and so are susceptible to survey by aerial photography, geophysics, and surface collection.

In the Republic of Ireland, highways are constructed by the National Roads Authority (NRA), which also takes responsibility for steering the routes as far as possible so as to avoid the destruction of cultural assets—including archaeological deposits and historic buildings. In 2004, the NRA, with Meath County Council, proposed to construct the M3 motorway from Clonee to Kells, a scheme that would result in 110 km of road and affect 700 ha of land (NRA 2005). They began by commissioning archaeologists to carry out desktop assessments locating the major monuments and likely deposits, and then proposed ten possible routes for the motorway and sent them out for comment. The Orange and Green routes raised many objections, since they passed close to the Hill of Tara, one of Ireland's most significant historic places. Objections, which included comments solicited and received from archaeologists in other countries, not only focused on damage to particular sites on the route, but cited the detrimental visual impact on Tara's landscape. This was partly an aesthetic value, but it was also based on research needs: it was felt that if the road were in the wrong place, the prehistoric landscape could never again be appreciated.

From this consultation process, the Blue route (B2) emerged as the preferred route, since it passed by on the far side of an existing road flanking the Hill of Tara. An environmental impact assessment design was then drawn up for B2 that recommended degrees of archaeological testing over five zones. Two known monuments lay on the route, and fifteen more sites had been found from artifact scatters and surface indications. Geophysical surveys were carried out over the entire B2 corridor. In Zone 2, a rapid gradiometer survey along transects spaced 10 m apart located 30 areas of high response, which were then surveyed with a magnetometer at $1 \times 0.5$ m intervals. This located 6 definite sites and 23 possibles. In Zones 1 and 3–5, magnetometer and magnetic susceptibility surveys along parallel strips 9 m wide and 11 m apart located 64 possible sites. Test trenching was then employed to verify the presence of sites and check blank areas. Trenches 2 m wide were opened along the center line of the roadway; and perpendicular to this axis, trenches every 20 m reached to the limits of the land-take on either side. The trenches were opened by mechanical excavator to below the surface deposit and then excavated by hand. Some 300 km of trenches were cleaned to subsoil in this way (a 10% sample). Over the whole route, 160 sites were located, varying in size from a single pit to a complex of enclosures, and in date from the Neolithic (5th–3rd millennia BC) to the 20th century, fairly typical of the densities encountered in Ireland. A preliminary list of sites by period and sector was issued, and then specifications were drawn up for the detailed examination of the sites that lay on the route—that is, the "mitigation strategy." NRA decided to incorporate their mitigation projects into an integrated research program before constructing the road. Investigation would include the assessment of landscape, palaeoecological research, excavation, and historical research. *After* sites were excavated, NRA expended yet more resources on large-scale geophysical survey of the vicinity, in order to put the excavated site into context.

The ultimate aim of the M3 Archaeological Research Framework was to transform the data generated on the M3 archaeological excavations from "information" to "knowledge" (NRA 2005; University College Dublin 2006; *www.m3motorway.ie*). This must constitute one of the most thorough and sensitive archaeological responses to a new road ever undertaken; for NRA, mitigation meant a great deal more than the creation of a record: newly uncovered features were placed in their palaeoenvironmental and historical context and the results widely disseminated (Deevy and Murphy 2009, 60).

Even with good support like this, European archaeologists are aware that standard responses will not necessarily find all the sites. For example, at Poses on the terrace of the River Seine in France, the Neolithic settlement excavated by Françoise Bostyn was betrayed by no air photograph and no surface pottery: it was buried under a meter of silt thrown up by the river. In this case, a great deal depended on the local amateurs who doggedly stayed loyal to the venture, as the professionals, with their gadgets, came and went. At their insistence, the site was eventually found by machine-trenching, which led to the recognition of a buried occupation surface. This was uncovered with massive earth shifting, and only then could the buildings be excavated in plan (Bostyn 2004).

Similarly, the LBK site at Geleen-Janskamperveld in Holland was anticipated through piecemeal observation by a local enthusiast, Harry Vromen, who noted Neolithic pottery in the fields in 1979 and tracked it intermittently in the sewer trenches and building sites of his home town (Geleen) for over a decade (Van de Velde 2007). Moreover, in spite of an advanced cultural heritage management system run by a sensitized government service, it still fell to Harry Vromen in 1989 to insist that the proposed expansion of Geleen in a northerly direction would destroy a large Neolithic settlement. New building had already started when Vromen invited a group of teachers to witness an LBK house being flooded with concrete. In 1991, the 3.5 ha out of the 5 remaining at that point were formally excavated in area by Leendert Louwe Kooijmans, with the participation of a small professional team and more than 100 students. More than 60 LBK house plans were recorded, with a wealth of pottery and flint (Van de Velde 2007, 15, 34). As at Poses, the difficulty of feature definition and its poor susceptibility to early warning derive largely from the terrain. Here the loess was covered in a thick layer of clay, with the LBK features cut through both. The clay had cracked during an ancient exposure, introducing numerous fissures, and this was covered in turn by colluvium, flooding in from the adjacent river. This undulating system had then been rendered perfectly flat by plowing, so that loess, clay, and colluvium all showed in bands where they had been truncated. During excavation, the house features—post-holes and quarry pits—showed differently at different levels due to truncation of the Neolithic ground surface and the diverse subsoils (Van de Velde 2007, 24–25). The terrain thus affected the archaeologists' appreciation of the final quantity and dimensions of the houses, as well as their ability to find the settlement in the first place. A large workforce was required to match the terrain to the opportunity that presented itself, and to the objectives, which were to map all the households of a Neolithic settlement and to study the social relationships between them. The use of test pits might have succeeded in registering the site-formation process, but little else.

One of the goals of this chapter, and of this book as a whole, is to urge that even where we know how to find sites, we must insist on an individual design that adequately profits from previous experience—"to find out what you don't know, using what you do know" (p. 26). While still on the gravel, we could look way back, half a century, to an excavation that in my view remains exemplary and instructive, Hope-Taylor's investigation of cropmarks at Yeavering (1977). To say it was ahead of its time is an understatement—it seems to have got steadily more in advance of its time as the lessons Hope-Taylor learned there—well documented, incidentally, in his chapter 3—have been forgotten elsewhere in the interests of "professional" speed and economy.

The settlement was located with a clear aerial photograph showing the imprint of rectangular halls. But when Hope-Taylor removed the topsoil and cleaned the surface of the sandy gravel, he was initially very surprised to see nothing at all—so he set about the task of making the invisible visible. He cleaned the surface not with trowels but stiff brushes, flicking the wrist so that the stones stayed in place but the lighter sand was removed, "like using a thousand tiny trowels," in his phrase (pers. comm.). This operation was time sensitive; the fills soon dried to the same color as their surroundings, and sand blew back to cover them up. Accordingly, he would brush a large enough area to see the straight lines of buildings—about 30 × 20 m—and then wait for rain— usually not long in coming in autumn in Northumberland. Then he would go up his two-story tower, reinforced against the winds, and wait. As the site dried, differentially, various aspects of the architecture would show briefly and could be captured on camera (FIG. 4.7).

a

FIGURE 4.7. (*a*) Yeavering, Northumberland, England. Brian Hope-Taylor's primary horizontal section after brushing, prolonged rain, and a strongly drying wind; with (*b*) the tower used (Hope-Taylor 1977, pl. 13, 17) (*HMSO, reproduced under UK Open Government Licence*).

b

Inside the foundation trenches thus revealed, he coaxed a story of use from the shadow of each timber post. Not by taking it apart as single contexts—where it would just collapse, in any case—but by studying it and dissecting it, looking from the top, from the side, measuring and thinking, and incorporating his interpretations into his drawings. It took him several years to excavate a dozen buildings, even though he already knew they were there. It wasn't a matter of labor; what was needed was thinking time, time to experiment. No vanished timber buildings, before or since, have had their history written with such exquisite precision as did Hope-Taylor in the 1950s. And yet for the next 25 years, the establishment, including Wheeler, ignored him.

This is the standard that should be emulated in our research and mitigation projects, but rarely is. Is thinking a luxury? The field-walking, trenching, and stripping we use on road schemes will often be inadequate and we know this; we are under pressure from shortage of time and not enough money. But let's keep the possibility of a more intensive level of recovery on the table, and more ingenious, more inquiring methods up our sleeves for the future. I'm optimistic that every year we will enlarge the repertoire of what the past has left us, because every year scientific archaeology improves. All we need is the political will to apply it.

## WET EUROPE

Since wetland is an extreme form of terrain, and as much part of the field archaeologist's theater of operations as the land, we should pay it a brief visit too. In a pioneering venture, Aidan O'Sullivan and his team surveyed the Shannon estuary as part of the Irish Discovery Programme's North Munster Project to locate sites in the mudflats exposed between high and low tide. During the exercise, previous archaeological finds, early maps, and place-names were collected and assessed. Great use was also made of early paintings and photographs, which provided evidence of the extensive fish-traps and other works of which now only intermittent timbers might remain. The initial survey was conducted by walking through the thick mud of the intertidal zone, most easily accessible for three weeks each year (in August or September). Some sites were only visible for two to three hours over ten to fifteen days a year. Archaeologists reached the foreshore by walking across the fields and searched the mudflats in sectors. Standard field-walking methods, using straight transects 20 to 30 m (66–98 ft) apart, were initially applied but soon abandoned: "after the first season in 1992 it was patently obvious that imposing an abstract field-walking grid on the Shannon estuary was exhausting, pointless and even dangerous. Frequently, we would have to walk through very soft muds to keep this grid system going, often sinking up to our thighs in deep muddy silts" (A. O'Sullivan 2001). Experience showed that the more productive (and safer) firm, eroding clays could be recognized by their dark color from a distance, and the archaeologists followed these with the retreating tide and returned before its advance. Important safety measures for the program included a thorough knowledge of the tides to avoid getting cut off, and loose rubber boots which could easily be kicked off, allowing an archaeologist to crawl to safety in the event of sinking in a mud pocket. The mudflats could be approached from the water by inflatable boat, but then visibility was limited to the area near the waterline.

Sampling methods included coring with a narrow auger or monolith tin, and subsequent analysis examined the stratification, pollen, diatoms, and foraminifera. Samples of wood pieces were taken for purposes of identification, studying carpentry, radiocarbon dating, and dendrochronology. Discoveries over the fourteen weeks of fieldwork included a submerged Neolithic forest, a Bronze Age house, and numbers of medieval and post-medieval fish-traps. Four of the fish-traps were subsequently excavated as part of the project. Archaeologists worked on the traps as they were exposed daily for two to three hours over a four-day period.

At a subsequent survey in the River Barrow, project director Aidan O'Sullivan was able to record 48 sites over 14 km (8.7 miles) in one day using binoculars from a decked boat. In the light of this experience, he proposed a three-stage process for estuary fieldwork, beginning with a rapid waterborne survey identifying potentially productive zones from timber traces or areas of the harder eroding clays (reconnaissance), followed by a second stage in which areas showing potential are targeted by foreshore-walking with a handheld GPS (evaluation). The third stage consists of the sampling of selected sites, making use of a rigid inflatable boat to provide access and transport (A. O'Sullivan 2001).

In the Lac de Paladru near Grenoble, southeast France, the team had to go beneath the surface and dig in the murky water (Colardelle and Verdelle 1993). At the medieval site, known as Charavines, posts had already appeared in dry seasons, and the village was covered by little more than 1 m of water. It was, however, exceptionally muddy, and excavation was largely by feel. To see sufficiently to locate objects, posts, and planks, excavators employed the so-called Swiss curtain, a device that pumped a linear current of freshwater to move away the silt as it was disturbed. Because of poor line-of-sight visibility, the excavators designed a grid of equilateral triangles made of wood that bolted together, and gradually crept out over the lake bed. Samples of sediment stratification were taken at every junction and were pulled out as cores using air balloons. Excavators extracted a huge yield of artifactual and environmental data, made a large map of planned houses, and obtained lots of good dates: here their ingenuity triumphed over a difficult terrain with zero visibility, and this village has understandably become a type site in the early history of feudal France.

## URBAN EUROPE

Sites in living towns that have to be excavated in advance of development have seen some of the most original and successful responses to the challenge of rescue. There have also, of course, been a series of disasters, where intervention took place too late, or too messily, to be useful. In some cases, the last minute reaction was heroic, as in the example of the *Dover* boat, which can serve as one incident on behalf of many. The Dover link road joining the Eastern Docks to the Channel Tunnel (A20) in Kent was due to run along the foreshore of the Channel, cutting through the silted estuary of the River Dour and through most of the maritime quarters of the old medieval and post-medieval town. However, when plans for the road were laid in 1991, there was no archaeological program in place. An impact assessment was hastily prepared by Canterbury Archaeological Trust's Keith Parfitt and accepted by the government agencies building the road, which provided access, time, and funds for the archaeological observation of the road line. Owing to the lateness of the provision, no research program was possible, and Parfitt's small mobile team intervened "on an opportunistic basis" along the 2 km long, 500 m wide road corridor for the next 30 months.

In September 1992, contractors sinking a coffered shaft 5 × 6 m in area to house a pump for an underpass encountered the medieval sea wall, which was avoided, and the timbers of a Roman harbor front, which were removed. Beneath this were seen more ancient timbers, at first thought to belong to a Roman boat; closer inspection in situ revealed a semicircular wooden block typical of a Bronze Age cleat. Although the contractors were already 19 weeks behind schedule, they agreed to suspend work for six days while the remains of one of the earliest boats in Europe were examined, 6 m below the street. The site was also 3 m below the level of the modern high tide, so continual pumping was required. Equipped with floodlighting, the team worked for 67 hours from midday on Monday, 28 September, to the following Sunday evening. Since there was no chance of re-siting the pumping station, the timbers were recorded in situ and then cut into 32 pieces with a diamond-tipped rotary saw and lifted on cradles.

It was quickly recognized that the length of the boat continued into an adjacent area. Its long-term future was uncertain, and the research rewards of finding the end of the boat were considerable. Accordingly, the state agencies ordered the sinking of another coffered area (Coffer Dam II) south of the first (Coffer Dam I), and a time of ten days was allowed for its investigation. The contents were removed by machine to a depth of 5 m over an area 5 × 7 m. Layers of beach shingle were removed by hand, and the excavators were delighted to find that the new area indeed contained one end of the boat. The boat pieces were freed from the sediment into which they had been pressed by 6 m of deposit (and a road) by mining a slot for the support plank with a jet of water and cutting gently with a thin blade. Experiments with other methods such as undersailing with planks or steel plates had proved damaging. Each section of timber was marked with a code letter and a north sign. The pieces were placed in storage tanks prior to long-term conservation and reassembly. Excavators recorded 9.50 m of the boat, which was radiocarbon dated to ca. 1500 cal BC (Clark 2004).

This kind of courageous intervention is admirable, and we should not cavil at the way research, in the end, proved decisive over conservation. In pursuit of a more orderly procedure, the profession has invested heavily in predictive methodologies, so that the archaeological riches are evident in advance. Having said that, undocumented occupation 6 m down under a modern town will always be hard to anticipate. Where predictive mapping has been undertaken, the effect has been to emphasize the astonishing variety of the deposits encountered under towns: wet, dry, beautifully articulate, and hopelessly jumbled (Carver 1983; 1993).

In spite of this variety, British urban excavators in particular have been champions of a standardized method, but it is not difficult to find the main roots of this practice; it lies neither in research questions nor in the terrain, but in the social context. The need for certainty was evident among the archaeological companies, as well as among developers and planners. The cost of real estate in towns is inflated, and the time is short; so with a market price determined by the developer through competitive tender, the newly formed profession must defend its livelihood, and the quality of the work, against cut-price contractors. The single-context system thus emerges as a minimum standard (Roskams 2001). This is understandable and has resulted in the acceptance of the archaeological mission within the building trade. But it is not always an appropriate way of doing research, and the danger is that the design stage is omitted altogether, even when given lip-service.

The scene can improve with only a slight change of attitude, where urban archaeology is accepted not as a minimal response, but as a procedure for negotiating a research opportunity. With sufficient social and government support, this can happen even in a high-pressure development. For example, an agreement signed in 1983 to build line D of the Lyon metro (underground railway) included within it a designed archaeological project. Set-piece excavations were planned at Place Bellecour, Le Vallon Gorge-de-Loup, and in quartier Saint Jean. Site monitoring was planned at the bridge of La Guillotière, but was later expanded into a large excavation, richly informed by archive work, after the bridge had been demolished (Burnouf et al. 1991). At Saint-Jean, director Françoise Villedieu's preferred excavation strategy was to lay the full 1,100 m$^2$ area open at the same time, in order to improve her chances of understanding it. However, the need to keep traffic moving, and the need for space to accommodate the back-dirt pile, meant that the area had to be dug in three bites. Selectivity was applied through recovery levels (some sectors dug faster than others). Recording priority was given to the stratigraphic sequence, using a hierarchical system of stratigraphic units in which contexts, rooms and walls, had separate number series. The records generated comprised 2,350 record cards, 450 plans, 2,500 photographs, and more than 100,000 finds, including 189 coins. The excavation was completed on time, and four months were allowed to put the records in order. The finds took another 22 months to sort, and a seriation of Roman pottery was used to help order the contexts and features for which the stratification was poor or cut off from the main sequence. This enabled a full site model to be prepared, one that answered the Roman question (the site was occupied from the 2nd century) and much else besides. The bridge at La Guillotière was demolished at the time of the metro construction, and proved to be a multiperiod monument. Area excavation was negotiated at the bridgehead, involving the exposure of deposits extending over 3,500 m$^2$ and 15 m deep, provided that this did not hold up construction. The archaeologists lamented the lack of a prior evaluation, which would have helped to design a program "to understand better, therefore dig better, a type of deposit not confronted before." They soon encountered over 4,000 timber piles supporting piers that had been refurbished on many occasions, and immediately developed their project in two directions. First they launched a program of dendrochronology: 700 timber piles were sampled by sawing off a horizontal slice, and 122 (3% of the total) were used to create a dendrochronological sequence which ran from AD 945 to 1721. The second initiative was to appoint a full-time archivist, who, armed with the first dendro dates, could seek out historical contexts in which the Rhône bridge would have been rebuilt.

No-one would say this was a perfect project, but what stands out is the determination of the archaeologists to make research out of the opportunity and negotiate to that purpose at every turn. It is clear that urban deposits are full of surprises, and it is this that can freeze the relationship with developers. Some of this uncertainty can be removed through better evaluation, but it must be observed that even if the evaluation cannot predict everything (and it never can), a transparent procedure of evaluation and design qualifies the archaeologists to be members of the broader development team, especially if they declare their purpose to be the generation of specified new history. Ironically, accepting an archaeological design, integral with the rest of the project, makes it easier for developers to vary the program in the event of surprising finds, unlike the old-fashioned prescription of "preservation by record," conducted under access granted for a fixed period.

## MONUMENTAL EUROPE

We stay in France for my last port of call, but with a complete change of subject: an example of how fine fieldwork can be marred, or even mired, by an excess of philosophizing. Really, all archaeological investigators need is good design, good implementation, and the humility to admit that they can only do their best for their age. We are not gods. At Table des Marchands, Serge Cassen investigated a famous megalithic tomb and stone row in Brittany, having taken over direction from another archaeologist, Jean L'Helgouac'h. Both did an excellent job. There were three campaigns, of which the first can be regarded as reconnaissance—in this case of the monument as it had survived—the second as evaluation and design, and the third as implementation. Most of the deposit consisted of stone rubble and debris left by previous excavators or vandals, but the archaeologists soon learned to distinguish between episodes. They found some strata preserved against the footings of the enormous stone foundations and used 92 small sections to indicate a sequence. They defined holes that had once held standing stones or stelae, and traces of earlier occupation underneath the rubble cairn. Other indications came from the reuse of broken stone slabs in the construction of the tomb. The story line was presented in convincing digital imagery: In

Phase 1, a magnificent stone row stood, including the famous Grand Menhir. In Phase 2, the row fell over, probably due to an earthquake. In Phase 3, a chambered tomb (the so-called Table des Marchands) was built at the same site, recycling some of the pieces of menhir. In Phase 4, a new tomb, the Er Grah, was constructed; and in Phase 5, the site was abandoned.

The author and most recent excavator, Serge Cassen, does not spare his predecessor, who is referred to intermittently with clenched teeth through the 900-page report (2009). He asserts that 5–10% of records had been lost; bemoans the specialist who deserted him for a job in Paris "which was all very nice for him"; and most curiously berates the publisher for insisting on a synthesis. Now why would an excavator object to that? In spite of a generous dollop of postmodernist musing, the writing of a synthesis apparently embarrassed him because it might not prove always to be right. But surely a student of Foucault, Derrida, or Bourdieu, as he assures us he is, would not expect to be right about anything, only to unveil his hidden agenda. It is sad to see a really great project inhibited by such trivia. Of course, every report ever written may prove to be wrong. *Et alors?* It is, however, our bounden duty to state what we believe the site meant, in our terms, in our day. Being wrong later is what keeps the party going.

## Conclusion

Back from our tour, we can see that none of the archaeologists we have encountered actually applies a standardized method, even when they claim to. Far from there being a justification for exporting a standard method from one country to another, there is virtually no occasion when a method can be automatically applied for a second time, unless it is at the site next door to the one before. So let's agree that field archaeology has no place for methodological dogma. Each project represents a solution to the problem of posing questions to strata in different terrains and often in different social arenas. These solutions are ingenious, original, and deploy a multiplicity of techniques. Our fallback procedures—box excavation, area excavation, single-context planning, the Harris matrix, even stratigraphic approaches—are always waiting in the wings, but in the event may play a relatively small role. Other practices come to the fore, as they are justified and adapted, through design, to the job in hand.

Currently, as this brief excursion shows, there is a geographical pattern of preferred method (Fig. 4.8). An excavators' map of the world—admittedly a bit impressionistic—shows stratigraphers in Britain and in western and northern

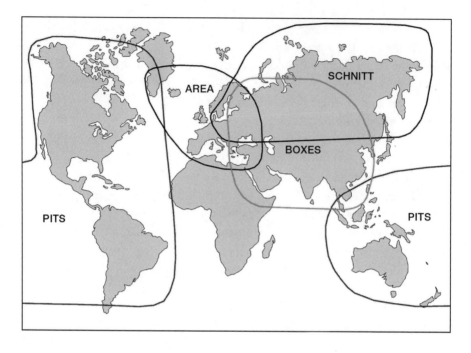

FIGURE 4.8. Pit, box, schnitt, and area; some (approximate) zones of preferred use (*map by the author*).

Europe and some ex-British colonies; test-pitters in United States and the Pacific; *schnitters* in Germanic Europe; and boxers in China. This distribution could have a historical explanation—a combination of diffusion and local conditions, like the prehistoric diffusion of wheat or spinach. But its relation to design is harder to understand. The *terrain* is not exclusively calling the shots; for example, test pits are widely used over very different types of ground. Some areas, like the eastern Mediterranean, seem more ready to try everything, though I would not deny here the influence of many international teams working in proximity to one another. Different methods, it seems, are sometimes applied to the same terrain, while some strong characters, particularly Britons and Americans, apply the same method whatever the terrain and whether it works or not.

There is more of a case for associating a method with a *social context*; for example, the box system suits nations with a currently low ratio of skilled to unskilled labor, as in India and China. The test pit is attractive to those who have virtually only skilled labor—a small number of experts on site, as with American academics and commercial firms. Open-area stratigraphic archaeology requires a large skilled labor force, ideally augmented by dedicated volunteers. It is extremely expensive compared with the others, and at its most useful when detailed research questions meet well-defined strata—as in the European town.

Since the practice of field archaeology is imprisoned in the local system that funds it, this map of practice may be slow to change. *Prima facie* it would be highly desirable—for a subject that fancies itself as an international discipline—to match archaeological practice to problems on the ground rather than resign them to a deep-rooted national default system. Terrain and social context clearly vary, and greatly influence what is done from country to country, so that each country acquires a history of its own making. Does this variation matter? If archaeology is a national indulgence, clearly not. Like cooking, history can even have a certain ethnic charm. But if a nation claims that its research agenda is a local matter and determines its practice in the field, this leaves the global discipline in irons, a political as well as an economic prisoner.

The question here is whether we are conscious of a world agenda for archaeology. If we are, then we have a basis for reconstructing the discipline so that it is led only by design and not by dogma or local custom. Drawing up the list of topics published in *Antiquity*, as I do each year, I am conscious of certain recurrent themes and trends. But, unfortunately, this agenda is not constructed in an even-handed manner. Earlier prehistory, with a focus on hominin dispersal, evolution, the emergence of symbolic practice, ritual, and social control, commands ubiquitous interest and is strongly scientific and international. Later prehistory becomes quite nationalistic, with tribes, peoples, and kingdoms driving the inquiry. Historic archaeology is split down the middle, with some looking for an international subject, such as "post-colonialism" or "people without history," and others championing national, regional, or local histories for reasons that have much to do with current rather than ancient affairs.

Sectional interests are reinforced among the young by governments and journals in the form of what is taught in university. Clearly this is part of a wider problem. How has the study of the experience of humans on earth become such a narrow, nationalist preoccupation? Whatever the cause, there is clearly something to be gained in confronting it by advancing a design-led field archaeology. If we return to our analogy with architecture, we could see field archaeology as a universal discipline—like architectural engineering, in which every river was crossed but crossed in a different way, using the best the discipline can offer, aligned with local conditions. Theoretical archaeology, on the other hand, remains more disputed, ephemeral, and unevenly distributed, like architectural aesthetics, and national interests may be served at a superficial, decorative level. If this is the case, then the question of a global agenda becomes redundant. We are builders of bridges and makers of roads, solvers of problems, creators of history. If we serve national pride, it is by showing that local stories matter to the rest of the world.

# CHAPTER 5

# FROM PROCUREMENT
# TO PRODUCT: A ROAD MAP

## INTRODUCTION

I have tried to convince you that archaeological investigation addresses a wide range of opportunities through a wide range of designs; that its inquiries operate at a wide range of scales from mega to nano, with a big and varied scientific tool kit, and that our real contribution to society, our product, is new knowledge. The profession hasn't quite accepted the first of these contentions, and the legislature hasn't quite accepted the last. Moreover, in deregulated countries we currently operate in two sectors, one in universities, privileging ideas and ignoring conservation, and the other in commercial companies, paid to record sites rather than research them.

Now I want to propose a remedial strategy: a procurement procedure that can unify both sectors and serve their publics. Design will be the common principle for both our sectors. Design is the way the public measures our value, it is our badge of office, our passport into the boardroom and the planning office. Design reconciles our objectives, the terrain, and the social context in which we work, so as to get the best outcome for our day and for the future. Design drives projects the world over, even where it is not admitted. And where the opportunity for design is frustrated, it still lurks beneath the surface of the mind of the practitioner, awaiting release.

There are three parts to the argument. The first is descriptive: we shall look at what field archaeologists do, their *procedure* presented as six consecutive stages, each with a different mission. Behind this staged procedure is a particular way of thinking, or theoretical framework, and this *theory* will be given an airing in part 2. As we will see, the idea of a linear process driven by design, which is what I embrace, flies in the face of current academic fashion, which is for a circular or hermeneutic reasoning. By contrast, the various procedures used in the public sector are linear, for the good reason that money is being paid and a product expected. The particular horse I am backing also runs a straight race, and my belief is that this is the way to carry research to a successful conclusion, whether in the university or the commercial sector. This is the focus of the last part of the argument, part 3. Assuming a linear itinerary is accepted, what form should it take, and can we achieve the objective of adopting a single procedure and protocol for the *procurement* of both academic and commercial ventures?

## FIELD RESEARCH PROCEDURE (FRP)

First, to present (briefly) a staged procedure for fieldwork, I suggest what goes into each stage and show how design fits in and moves the procedure forward. In my scheme, *reconnaissance* defines sites and landscapes, *evaluation* gives them their current value, *project design* determines what to do, *implementation* does it, *analysis* makes sense of the results, and *publication* stores and disseminates the results and their interpretations in the public domain (Carver 2009, fig. 2.9; here FIG. 3.5).

*Reconnaissance* techniques include aerial survey, from a plane or a satellite, and surface survey, picking up pottery and plotting it on a map. The output of the reconnaissance phase can be a set of pre-identified sites—hillforts of the Danube, say, or a total survey of one area, a valley or moorland or desert. The process may be thought of as the making of an inventory. In most countries, reconnaissance is continuous and fed into a centralized database that becomes the archaeological memory for a territory. In a perfect world (the one we don't live in), this archive collects all the records of demolished houses and treasure hunters' loot, as well as the observations of the enthusiast. It is the empirical resource, which for many constitutes archaeology's true rationale. Petrie had an ambitious vision for such a thing in 1904: "A square mile of land, within an hour's journey of London [of course], should be secured; and built over with galleries at the rate of 20,000 square feet a year, so providing 8 miles of galleries 50 feet wide in a century, with room yet for several centuries of expansion at the same rate" (Petrie 1904, 133). This was clearly a man who had a lot of digging in mind.

In *evaluation*, the task is to examine a particular area of ground and give it value, and the principal way we have come to do that is to peer beneath the surface and produce a predictive model of what lies in store. This is a deposit model, sometimes called a "resource model" (especially in the case of landscapes). The last 30 years have seen lots of research and development on deposit-modeling techniques, especially those that don't destroy strata. As noted in Chapter 2, geophysics continues to develop and indeed must do so further. Low-impact, high-resolution remote mapping techniques, whether alone or in combination, provide our best chance of composing productive designs and getting a seat at the table at the earliest stages of the negotiation of a site's future.

Sadly, we are usually obliged to rely on something much more crude: an array of test pits or a set of trenches, of which the kindest thing to say is that the vision they afford is limited. In towns, that vision is often sufficient: it measures the depth and quality of strata, essential for an excavation design; but here we are not wondering where the site is, since it is the town itself. In the countryside, the pitting or trenching is born of two contradictory desires—one to make sure nothing is missed, and the other to do it using as few people as possible. This is the preferred response of the profession, which is short of time and money and nervous about whether to believe remote mapping. While a test pit tells you little about the past, it does serve evaluation in indicating the character of the deposit at the sampled points—often suggestive enough to promote a more thorough response. Archaeologists know that test pits can never be guaranteed to represent all there is, however they are laid out (see, e.g., Balkansky et al. 2000; Burger et al. 2004; Hey 2006). If, for purposes of costing, the area to be examined is set at a standard (say 15%), the result is a self-fulfilling prophecy, as 85% of the area to be investigated will be written off. If nothing was found in the 15% examined, then nothing is what there will always be, since all the deposit will be removed to build a road. In Europe, "nothing" is hardly ever a credible verdict, wherever you are. As already suggested, the existence of archaeological deposits depends not on whether you can see them, but on how hard you look. The test pit and trial trench make random contacts with macroscopic strata, damage much, understand little. To propose that the hit rate is a function of the layout of trenches (Verhagen and Borsboom 2009) is simply cod science; it depends what's down there.

What is to be done? First, improve remote mapping, invest in its development, improve confidence in its outcome, both in our own and in associated professions. Second, improve the certainty of detection by using strip-and-map techniques. In this method, following surface assessment, the whole of the topsoil in removed by machine and the palimpsest beneath is cleaned (FIG. 1.4). At this horizon and at this scale, most archaeological features are visible, or can be enhanced using water, a photographic tower (e.g., FIG. 4.7), and geophysics (operating with greater sensitivity beneath the topsoil). There are exceptions, of course, and we met one in the last chapter, where Neolithic houses were buried in a meter of alluvium (p. 106). But in general, at least on a flat site, strip-and-map gives us a greater appreciation of, and more certainty about, the archaeology about to be destroyed than would any number of trenches. Strip-and-map does not damage sites; if, in the event, the sites are not to be affected by a development, they can be covered over again, and we know exactly where they are. In fact, there are occasions when we would be right to insist on strip-and-map as a minimum prescription, and it need not cost more than trenching. The topsoil has to come off anyway, usually at the expense of the developer, so this is money saved by archaeology. The cleaning of areas, often vast, is obviously not practical for two or three people; but it would be for twenty or so; and these could be volunteers and students, people currently excluded from the mitigation process for reasons (such as health and safety) that are often exaggerated. The result of adopting the strip-and-map technique would be twofold: to answer the (just) criticism that we do not search as diligently for archaeology as we did twenty years ago; and to help repair the relationship between commercial archaeology, its associated professions, and its local voluntary supporters.

A modern evaluation project should not simply throw trenches across the landscape; it needs to match its methods to the terrain. This requires that the territory to be evaluated is first divided into designated zones, and each zone addressed with the appropriate method of sensing. In their study of the Middle Gila River in Arizona, Ravesloot and Waters (2004) took the surface geology as the basis of zonation and used the map of zones as a platform on which to plot site types. This gave a research result, but also showed a variation in visibility between periods, a typical outcome of evaluation. Only extensive exposure can offer a reliable preview of a deposit. Test pits and trenches don't; the problem is often that we never knew they didn't.

## PROJECT DESIGN

Design puts in an appearance before each stage of the field research procedure (FRP)—before reconnaissance, evaluation, implementation, analysis, and publication. In each case, we need a statement of what we intend to do, how long it will take, how much it will cost. All these design stages are important, but the design undertaken before implementation is paramount. This stage of field research is the most destructive, and its design—that is, the *project design*—determines the fate and future of the site or landscape under scrutiny.

So, what's in a project design (FIG. 5.1; Carver 2009, 335–361) and how does it come about? The premise is that it assesses three factors—objectives, terrain, and social context—and tries to match them. This is the input. The corresponding output from the design process must contain at least two programs—one serving research and one serving conservation—though it may contain much else. The *research program* is designed to generate new knowledge; the *conservation* (or *resource management*) *program* to protect what remains of the resource, below ground, above ground, and in the archive. The term "conservation" as used here simply refers to the need to conserve all undisturbed parts of a landscape, site, or building that retain research potential.

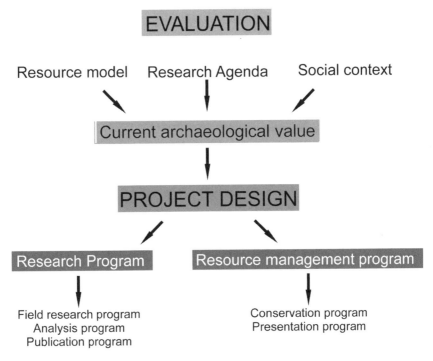

FIGURE 5.1. Project design: input and output (*diagram by the author*).

Thus, as far as possible, the design of a project incorporates the conservation in situ of any part of a deposit that is not to be dug (e.g., Arup 1991; English Heritage 1997, 2006; Historic Scotland 2003; and see p. 142). The way this is done may include piling, membranes and sealants, and administrative measures to minimize the effects of later land use. Management programs also include arrangements designed to allow access for visitors.

It is axiomatic in this approach that neither of these two programs is optional. Commercial archaeologists need to include research in their projects, but university lecturers need to include site management plans in theirs. Neither happens routinely at present. Some excavators have a blind spot to the conservation of sites and landscapes and imagine that it has little to do with them. For those working in the commercial sector there is some excuse, but there is none for researchers, especially those working in universities. The United Kingdom is peppered with the bleeding hulks of half dug sites. That is because even where there was a project design, it very rarely included a site management plan.

Notice that the matters input into the design—namely, objectives, terrain, and social context—are not strictly independent variables; each can cause a change in the other. We select our objectives according to what is possible. The terrain and the objectives suggest the workforce; but the social situation may not allow the chosen workforce to be deployed. The use of strip-and-map (above) provides an example: even when demanded by the objectives and the terrain, it is severely inhibited at present by restrictive practices and the exclusion of volunteers and students.

A project design does not have to include excavation; it may be just survey, though it does not have to include survey either. It may just propose conservation. But most often, if it gets this far, it is likely to include excavation, survey, the recording of standing buildings, and conservation measures. These together constitute the implementation of the project.

## IMPLEMENTATION

The implementation of a design comprises the execution of the two programs, including fieldwork and conservation measures (see FIG. 3.5). For that part of a project that requires excavation, we probably have the greatest difficulty deciding what to do in advance, because of the unpredictability of strata. I don't think this lets us off the hook. A good evaluation should provide a firm basis for planning what to do and where; and a good method of expressing these decisions in advance, costing them and controlling them during implementation, is the use of *recovery levels* (TABLE 5.1). Excavators always apply different levels of intensity to investigations on site, whether they admit it or not, and these imply different speeds of excavation, and so different costs. Thus recovery levels provide a vital instrument of design and subsequent control.

The recovery level system is as good a way as any of putting excavation techniques under rapid review (FIG. 5.2). Level A uses bulldozers, back-blading Drotts, and backhoes on wheeled excavators. These machines move much earth, but the level of definition is crude. Level A is used for the removal of topsoil or surface debris not thought to have much historical value. Level B uses picks, shovels, rakes, hoes, and so on. You see a bit more and achieve a bit more precision. You will find brick walls, pits, large features, and big artifacts, and will be able to locate them. It is used primarily to clear up after machining. Level C uses rapid troweling or brushing to clean up surfaces. Level D is more pernickety. It is used to define horizons with fine troweling and water spray. It is used to study features and take them apart. Level E is more delicate still and is applied especially to features of high historical yield, such as graves. The tool kit is as complex as a dentist's—and it is at Level E that all those micro and nano methods start to kick in.

Level F requires you to take a feature home and excavate it in the lab. The procedure has a fine pedigree—for example, Ivor Noel Hume lifting a 17th-century helmet at Martin's Hundred (1982, 180), or Dagmar Selling examining the burial chamber under Mound 2 at Högom in Medelpad, Sweden, in the early 1950s—way ahead of its time (Ramqvist 1992, 36–43). Once Selling realized the timber-lined tomb under Mound 2 was intact, she decided to lift it in a block and excavate it in the laboratory. The stony mound was recorded and removed, the wooden chamber was isolated and encased in steel shuttering, lifted by crane, and transported by lorry to the lab. There it was X-rayed and then excavated—upside down, as it happens—very carefully under controlled conditions, away from wind and blowing sand and meddling people.

The records generated on site are also closely related to the recovery levels—the most detailed recording being applied to the most detailed excavation. I challenge anyone to demonstrate that they do all parts of their excavation and recording at the same unbeatably high level of precision. Also to be noted here is that the records reflect the multiple concepts of on-site interpretation, giving us clear accounts of features and structures as well as contexts. And lastly, excavation and

## Table 5.1 Recovery levels

| LEVEL | COMPONENT | FIND | CONTEXT |
|---|---|---|---|
| A | (Not recovered) | Surface finds<br>PLOT in 2D | Inferred by sensor<br>OUTLINE PLAN |
| B | (Not recovered) | Large finds<br>RECORD EXAMPLES;<br>KEEP EXAMPLES. | Defined by shovel<br>DESCRIBE |
| C | (Not recovered) | All visible finds.<br>RECORD ALL. KEEP<br>EXAMPLES. MAY<br>PLOT BY m². | Defined by coarse trowel.<br>DESCRIPTION<br>(Munsell for mortars<br>and natural). |
| D | SAMPLE SIEVING<br>of spoil on site for<br>presence of specified<br>material (spoil not<br>kept) | All visible finds.<br>PLOT in 3D and KEEP<br>ALL. | Defined by fine trowel.<br>DESCRIPTION (incl.<br>Munsell).<br>PLAN 1:20. |
| E | TOTAL SIEVING<br>of spoil on site for<br>presence of specified<br>material and KEEP<br>SPOIL. | All visible finds.<br>PLOT in 3D and KEEP<br>ALL. | Defined minutely.<br>DESCRIPTION (incl.<br>Munsell).<br>PLAN (natural colour)<br>1:10 or 1:5 contour. |
| F | MICRO SIEVING.<br>Soil block in laboratory. | (as component) | (as LEVEL E)<br>and LIFT AS BLOCK |

FIGURE 5.2. Excavation methods applied at different recovery levels, in order of increasing precision (*all photos by the author*). (*a*): Level A: stripping topsoil with a hinged bucket.

## Table 5.1 Recovery levels (continued)

|   | FEATURE | STRUCTURE | LANDSCAPE | EXAMPLE |
|---|---------|-----------|-----------|---------|
| A | Inferred by sensor. OUTLINE PLAN. | Inferred by sensor. OUTLINE PLAN. | Inferred by sensor. | Field-walking |
| B | Defined by shovel. SHORT DESCRIPTION OUTLINE PLAN. | (as features) | PLOT STRUC-TURES on OS | 19th-century house |
| C | Defined by coarse trowel. FULL DESCRIPTION; DETAILED PLAN HEIGHT | Defined by coarse trowel. EXCAVATE AS ONE. PHOTOGRAPH. | 1:100 PLAN PROFILE | 16th-century pits |
| D | Defined by fine trowel. FULL DESCRIPTION. DETAILED PLAN 1:20 (color coded). CONTOURS. PHOTOGRAPH (B/W) | Defined by fine trowel. EXCAVATE AS ONE. PHOTOGRAPH by PHASE | 1:100 PLAN CONTOUR SURVEY | Timber trace building |
| E | Defined minutely. FULL DESCRIPTION PLAN (color) 1:10 or 1:5 CONTOUR. PHOTOGRAPH. | Defined minutely. EXCAVATE AS ONE. PHOTOGRAPH by PHASE | (as LEVEL D). CONTOUR SURVEY | Skeleton |
| F | (as LEVEL E) | (as LEVEL E) | (as LEVEL D) | Complex artifact |

FIGURE 5.2. (*cont.*) (*b*): Level B: shoveling out a ditch.

FIGURE 5.2. (*cont.*) (*c*): Level C: preparing a horizon and plotting finds.

FIGURE 5.2. (*cont.*)
(*d*): Level D: recording a pit.

FIGURE 5.2. (*cont.*)
(*e*): Level E: excavating
a burial.

FIGURE 5.2. (*cont.*) (*f*): Level F: lifting the contents of a grave as a consolidated block.

its recording itself should be monitored in a detailed, routinely written site journal. You will not pass this way again. This has always been the case on good research excavations—but it should be the case on all commercial excavations too.

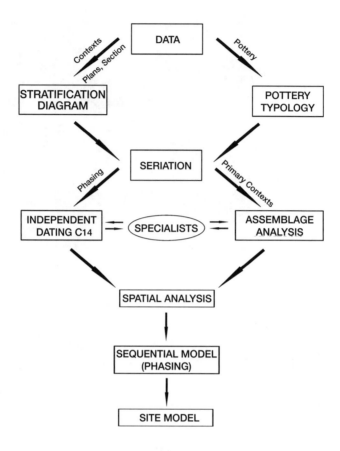

FIGURE 5.3. An analytical itinerary (*chart by the author*).

These records are then subject to *post-excavation analysis*, which can be thought of as three main programs—assemblage, space, and chronology—linked together in an *analytical itinerary* (FIG. 5.3; Carver 2009, 197–204). The outcome of the process is a site model, the coordinated, documented account of what happened where, at what date. This then attracts a commentary from the excavator, who compares it with other findings, analogies, and parallels to give us the richer kind of interpretation that we know as *synthesis*. If you find this nice and obvious, I am glad of it. It is a product, expected of us, I believe, when we work in the service of the research community, our sponsors, and the broader public. The product is delivered in the sixth stage, *publication*; but since we serve such a diverse group of customers, we must be ready to disseminate the same thing several times in different ways (TABLE 5.2; Carver 2009, 316).

Recently, a publication trend of great significance has arisen in Europe: the melding of the client report (no. 3) with the research report (no. 4). For example, Framework Ltd's published investigation at Stansted Airport offers a well-designed and accessible account of their findings in advance of runway construction, presenting different kinds of evidence together on the same page (Framework 2008). In one sector, they made use of excavated wall-lines to imply a hall building, and the distribution of animal bones showed that this building had attracted an unusual proportion of roe deer bones. The interpretation could step up a gear when they found that the part of the airport where they worked was still marked as a deer park on a map of 1777; and their hall building could become a hunting lodge. Other promising examples of generating good research

## Table 5.2. Modes of publication

| | |
|---|---|
| 1 | **FIELD REPORT:** Records made on site – written, drawn, photographic, digital, artifacts, samples; stored in museum |
| 2 | **LAB REPORT:** Analyses conducted – stratigraphic, spatial, artifacts, biota; posted online |
| 3 | **CLIENT REPORT:** Evaluation, survey, or excavation report in fulfillment of contract, usually in advance of disturbance or destruction of deposits; desktop-published copies, usually property of the client |
| 4 | **RESEARCH REPORT:** Report on field investigation and its local, regional, national, and international significance; subsidized multiple distribution as an article in peer-reviewed journals or as peer-reviewed monograph |
| 5 | **POPULAR BOOK:** Research report written by an archaeologist for the non-professional and aimed at the general public; published and distributed by a commercial publisher as a commercial proposition |
| 6 | **POPULAR MEDIA:** Reports in magazines, newspapers, radio, and television programs, usually featuring archaeologists but under the control of media editors and producers and aimed at the general public |
| 7 | **DISPLAY:** Exhibitions on site or in museums, promoted and fed by archaeologists but under the control of museum staff and/or designers; aimed at the general public |
| 8 | **PRESENTATION:** Preparation of an excavated site or building to provide for conservation of the remaining resource (conservation plan) and informed access for the general public (interpretation plan) |

SOURCE: After Carver 2009, 316.

from mitigation opportunities will be found in the syntheses drawn from several interventions published by NRA in Ireland (e.g., Deevy and Murphy 2009) or INRAP (Institut National de Recherches Archéologiques Preventives) in France (e.g., Catteddu 2009).

## SOME THEORETICAL ASPECTS OF THIS FRAMEWORK

Notice that each stage of this procedure is defined by its purpose, what it sets out to do—not by its techniques. The techniques serve the purpose. It's true that reconnaissance mainly makes use of landscape survey, and evaluation of site survey; but a modern project makes use of survey and excavation, pollen sampling, and much else in its implementation phase. Some textbooks tell you that surveys are "preliminary to excavation." This is not the case. Survey may appear at every stage in the course of an investigation, which may or may not include excavation

My own inspiration for this procedure came from the army, which taught me in the form of the mnemonic *SMEAC*: situation, mission, execution, administration, and communications—the components of the army's equivalent of the project design—that is, the battle plan. As I eventually discovered, FRP wasn't an original contribution to archaeological method, even in the 1970s, but there were differences. Charles Redman and the processualists also advocated a staged procedure (Redman 1973; 1987). David Clarke offered us an itinerary for his analytical archaeology of dazzling complexity (Clarke 1968, 36). For Lewis Binford, this way of thinking was essentially scientific, and archaeology was essentially a scientific pursuit. In 2001, he was still insisting that all research ideas in archaeology start and end with archaeological material: on their own, the humanities were incapable of framing and testing an idea (Binford 2001). He was effectively taken to task by George Odell in "Research Problems R Us," beginning with Binford's own famous phrase: "I could search for many years without finding a proposition with which I disagree more completely." Odell came out on top of this clash of titans, by showing that the humanities were just as capable—and indeed well practiced—in arguing from facts (Odell 2001). Robert Sharer and Wendy Ashmore were more explicit about the stages, calling the implementation stage "data acquisition"—it thus led logically to analysis (Sharer and Ashmore 1979, 534). They also explained their cycle of reasoning for which the field procedure was the active arm. Unlike *SMEAC*, the processualists saw archaeological thinking as cyclical, with the results of one inquiry being fed back into the next (FIG. 5.4).

Although reflexive archaeology was supposed to do something new, it actually took over the cyclical reasoning beloved of the processualists and elaborated it. Ian Hodder presented his version of the archaeological process: a hermeneutic circle, a continuous process of observation, interpretation, and looking again (FIG. 5.4a–c). The word "hermeneutic" has come to mean "to do with interpretation" and was used by Hodder to emphasize the idea that interpretation is never very far away from what we do on site (1999). That does not necessarily make it virtuous. Pedants will relish the fact that "hermeneutic" derives from the Greek god Hermes, who assisted the Fates in the composition of the alphabet, invented astronomy and weights and measures, and is well known for delivering arcane messages. Hermes is credited with many attributes, including ingenuity and theft, but clarity is not one of them. According to Robert Graves, when Hermes was appointed messenger of the

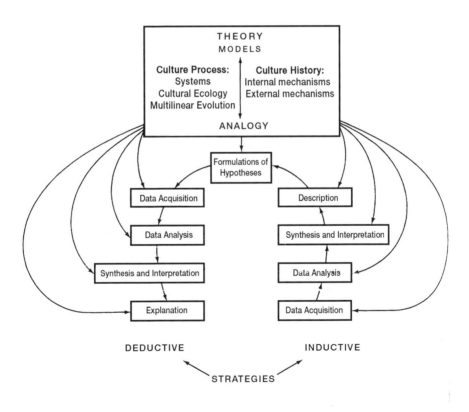

FIGURE 5.4. Cyclical thinking: (*a*): After Sharer and Ashmore 1979, 534 (*with permission*).

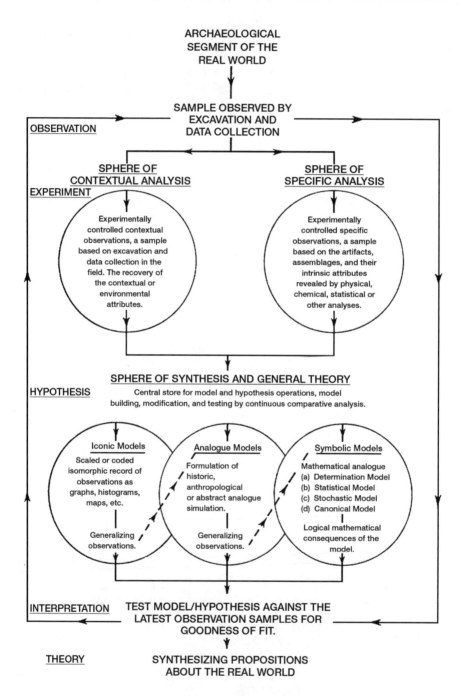

FIGURE 5.4. (*cont.*) Cyclical thinking. (*b*): After Clarke 1968, 36 (*with permission*).

gods, the following conversation took place on Olympus: Hermes said to Zeus, "Make me your herald and I will never tell lies, though I cannot promise always to tell the whole truth." And Zeus replies (with a smile), "That would *not* be expected of you" (Graves 1960, I, 65). As messengers go, this one seems somewhat unreliable.

Initially these spiraling schemes were meant to describe the long-term process of a researcher attempting to construct an adequate model of the past. They were not intended to be applied within a single project and do not provide very practical road maps for use in the field. Nor does championing the right to change one's mind with chronic frequency command much respect in our partner professions. As I envisage it, field research procedure should not be circular, but linear and proud of it; it starts in one place and finishes somewhere else. This gives the practitioner and the sponsor, and the whole of the society

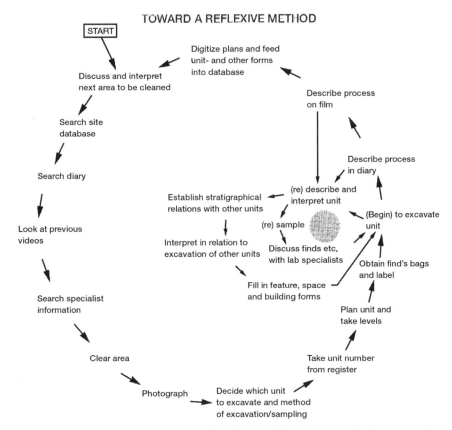

FIGURE 5.4. (*cont.*) Cyclical thinking. (*c*): After Hodder 1999, 102 (*with permission*).

they work for, a sense of achievement, an output, a product. I am happy to agree that the human brain likes to go round in circles, but I don't believe this is necessarily a good thing. It may be true of politics—but we don't like it in a novel and we find it exasperating in air travel. As we all know, archaeology destroys its own resource: we don't have the luxury of making endless hermeneutic visits to the same post-hole. Archaeological investigation is not a piece of private head-scratching but a public act of courage. Design epitomizes this courage: it requires you to say what you are going to do and then stick to it. If the design fails, you admit it and go home; you don't take revenge by flogging the site to death. If it succeeds, the results are entered into the database of archaeological knowledge, qualified by the way it was won. From this conclusion, which belongs to its day, new questions will arise, and new projects. This is the sense in which archaeological inquiry may be fed back and new journeys of research later undertaken. But we cannot undertake exactly the same journey twice, so it is essential that each one has its unique internal integrity.

However, the reflexive idea makes us think about the character of archaeological data and whether it was observable fact or evidence in the legal sense; and, if the latter, whether either the witness or the jury were to be trusted. The making of multiple models is one escape from the dilemma, pre-echoed for us in literature by such works as the *Alexandrian Quartet* or *The French Lieutenant's Women*, which offered different versions of the same events and allowed the reader as much agency as the author. The multiple-narrative can be seductive, because it doesn't oblige us to resolve any issues—events and explanations can remain "entangled," to use the current word—just like life. In the wrong hands, this can become dangerously purposeless and anti-scientific: a giant shrug of the shoulders, an inability to agree on a result and the consequent loss of support for archaeology from anyone spending money on it. There is a better and different, and much more positive take on the postmodernist position—namely, that what we can expect from archaeology are numerous small stories, including different stories about the same thing. This keeps intact the concept of a product—something we are giving the world, something we can stand beside as professionals—but at the same time allowing our product, the tale we tell, to be complex. To offer the exhilaration of complexity is not the same as putting a value on confusion.

We are now ready to tackle the last part of my argument: the case for an integrated design process that works equally well for the universities and the commercial sector. In Chapter 3, I suggested that deregulated societies have tended to split the archaeological world into two, so that researchers are paid to pursue one set of goals and the conserving profession another. This gives us another version of FRP, in which the practitioners follow parallel trajectories of equal importance but different emphasis. When we examine how design fits into field procedure, it is convenient to examine the research and the commercial itineraries separately. At present, they are like two DNA strands that have not worked out how to join into a double helix (see FIG. 3.5). We will see where they are different and where they are similar—and the message will be that they might one day merge.

## THE RESEARCH ITINERARY

How many research excavations do we know of that never got finished or written up? Rather a lot. That is because they never had a project design: they asked no questions, so got no answers, so there is nothing to publish. Although it is, in my view at least, self-evident that all field archaeology requires reconnaissance and evaluation stages, it has been something of a struggle to encourage research councils in Britain to accept the idea that projects must be first tested and designed before you support them. This may be because academics themselves have been very slow to understand what field archaeology does; they have kept their heads in the clouds, where the other academics are, and exchanged lofty flights of theory. But this is a bit like engineering taught by people who don't actually know how to build a bridge.

The rules for academics ought be the same as for everyone else once they get into the field. A full evaluation and project design should be required before starting any digging, and the proposed program must have a beginning and an end. Academics who say they will decide what to do when they get there, or will decide what happens in year 2 at the end of year 1, are acting unethically as well as illogically. Why would society release part of a precious resource to people who don't know what they intend to offer from it? Astonishingly, grant-giving bodies have actually encouraged this cavalier attitude by awarding grants on a seasonal basis: "Report back after the first season and then apply for a second season if the first was fruitful." Fruitful?! Archaeological field research is not the same as gathering whortleberries.

Research investigations, like any others, should be funded not by the year but by monitored stages: first an evaluation phase to develop the project; then the fieldwork; then the analysis; then the publication. This is still not routine in research councils, some of whom give out large sums of money for a lengthy project on the basis of a single application without a pilot study. Academics are expected to conceive an entire project and apply for money without any preparation apart from their own genius. Archaeological research is treated like history or physics; but it isn't like either. It has its own trajectory, one that involves prior reconnaissance and evaluation before a research program can be put together.

There is a certain amount of so-called scoping money in universities, where they cheerily call the process of project development "trailing a sprat to catch a mackerel." In other words, they give you a bit of money in the hope you will net a big grant for the university. But none of the national or international research councils known to me, or indeed the learned societies, seem to understand that archaeological investigation requires a feasibility study. In my experience of sitting on international panels, those in the know get local priming money from their universities or local societies and use it to prepare something resembling a project design, although it still rarely includes a conservation plan. Most countries have very little understanding of this mechanism, and the contrast is startling: their applications for money tend to take the form of wordy essays on the singular beauty of the site and its pottery and the near miraculous achievements of the applicant and his famous friends. They think they are doing history or art history. But the panelists, and especially the British and American panelists, are looking for something much more down to earth: evidence of a well-thought-out plan that will produce a novel and desirable outcome—in brief, evidence for a project design.

One has also to note that the research culture from the 1980s up to now has not favored systematically designed archaeological fieldwork. Western academics are assessed on the impact of their publications, and the assessment cycle is only five years long. This means offering something sharp or sugary rather than something solid that requires several years to digest. It is doubtful whether evaluation, and even some fieldwork, would be classed as research by universities. Best to publish something that is already accessible or, at most, do a couple of seasons picking up pottery—(but not too much of it). In these circumstances, academics are increasingly losing touch with the gathering of primary data.

So, by what procedure is the academic community best served? Although completed five years ago, Sutton Hoo offers a model that is still useful, and the implications of the unusual way this project was procured have not quite realized their full potential. A research group convened by the British Museum and the Society of Antiquaries of London got together, pledged some money for the further investigation of Sutton Hoo (the Anglo-Saxon royal burial ground in Suffolk), and put an advertisement in the *London Gazette* stating their intentions and inviting proposals from applicants. This was *de facto* a design competition. Proposals were duly submitted and a short list drawn up. Most applicants focused on the site and stated their desire to dig all of it. My application asked for a three-year period to conduct an evaluation and prepare a project design (Carver 2005, chaps. 2, 3).

In these three years, the appointed crew modeled the deposit, drew up a list of research topics, discussed them at three invitation seminars, and assessed the different kinds of public interest—our "social context." This included the local stakeholders who were to be represented by the so-called Sutton Hoo Society, formed especially for the purpose at a meeting in a local pub. The design included measures for public access and dissemination and the long-term management and protection of the site while it was being dug, and subsequently, the conservation plan.

The rationale for what was possible on the site was based on the visibility template—what could be seen, with which techniques, in which zones. This statement of what was possible was moderated by what was ethically desirable. So, for example, the excavation of the whole site would have been wrong, not just because it was illogical—we did not know what the "whole site" meant—but because it was unethical. The resultant research program consisted of an excavation supported by nested surveys—of the site locality, the Deben Valley, and three sample areas of East Anglia.

The project design was widely circulated and, in fact, published: a statement of what we intended to do, how much it would cost, and how long it would take. The fact that the proposed design was publicly presented before excavation started is possibly the single most important point to highlight here. The intention was to expose the plans to everyone who might have a stake in the outcome. It wasn't for the elite or the inner circle; it wasn't even for the government (although it was used to get scheduled monument consent). It was sent to universities at home and abroad, to archaeological societies, to the landowners, local residents, and to *Treasure Hunting Monthly*. It was, in fact, our version of what later became known as multivocality, but with this important difference: it was done in advance. Once it achieved consensus, this plan formed a "social contract" between the archaeological team and everyone else with an interest in the site; so it was important that it should not be subsequently varied: it wasn't ours to vary; the stakeholders now had ownership. It was also logical: once a building is going up, that is not the time to be changing the blueprint. There is an additional point at which practice modifies theory: Since our subject is socially embedded and we all get older and the world changes, there is no sense in proposing a project that lasts too long: the agenda, the objectives, the techniques, and the social context are all liable to change. In my view, a project starts to suffer from "concept fatigue" after about five years.

The Sutton Hoo Research Trust supported the design proposals and, with them, accepted the premise that they should be funded to completion. On that basis I began digging. With a three-year design phase, six years of digging, and thirteen years of analysis and publication (1983–2005), the inquiry was not unduly drawn out; nor did it cost a huge amount of money (about the same as one year's commercial excavation in London). But with a program lasting 22 years, there were few ways in which the project could be aligned with the university cycle of assessment which, in the United Kingdom, is focused on short-term output every five years rather than on long-term performance. Whether or not the assessment method is in need of reform, it would certainly help assessors of both university staff and research applications if primary research—that is, research in the field—were broken down into identifiable stages within a transparent itinerary.

## THE CRM ITINERARY

The idea of archaeological investigation needing a staged approach has been embraced with much greater enthusiasm by the commercial sector. In TABLE 5.3, we see two well-known itineraries—the US CRM procedure and the UK MAP2 (Management of Archaeological Projects, version 2) lined up side by side with FRP. I believe that, in general, these were all developed independently of one another; but this is not important. Three similar conclusions, however arrived at, must be good. Although not equally comprehensive, each itinerary expects stages to be preplanned, and the results of each stage to form the basis for the decisions of the next.

In England, MAP2 has been replaced by MoRPHE (Management of Research Projects in the Historic Environment), which is more complicated but more orientated toward research. In particular, MoRPHE introduces the enlightened idea that an archaeological company should be paid to develop a full project design before submitting it, something that research councils should adopt too (p. 86). The MoRPHE itinerary enriches FRP rather than

Table 5.3. Three linear itineraries for field investigation

| FIELD RESEARCH PROCEDURE (FRP) 1983 (Carver 2009) | CULTURAL RESOURCE MANAGEMENT, USA (CRM) (Neumann and Sanford 2001) | MANAGEMENT OF ARCHAEOLOGICAL PROJECTS, UK (MAP), ENGLISH HERITAGE 1991 (Andrews and Thomas 1995) |
|---|---|---|
| *Reconnaissance*<br>Inventory survey | Background<br>Surface survey<br>(Phase 1) | |
| *Evaluation*<br>Desktop assessment<br>Resource modeling<br>Research agenda | Evaluation (Phase 2) | *Appraisal*<br>Field evaluation |
| *Project Design*<br>Research program<br>Management program | Memorandum of<br>Agreement<br>Scope of work/<br>data Recovery plan | Project specification |
| Investigation | Data acquisition<br>(Phase 3) | Fieldwork |
| *Analysis*<br>Program design:<br>Analyses | | *Post-excavation assessment*<br>Analysis |
| *Publication*<br>Program design<br>Reports<br>Exhibition<br>Site presentation | | Archive<br>Publication |

enlarging it; it is more of a check-list detailing the management stages of any government-funded project: scope, assess, execute, output. It seems to me highly likely that these three versions will grow together until we can't tell them apart, carrying us from idea to output in a linear manner; each question becomes a project, each project gives an answer. For me, archaeological projects framed in this way give their practitioners a sense of achievement and their sponsors the impression of a job worth paying for. It only needs university research and the research councils to sign up to the same principles and we have made the integration happen. Or have we?

Clients—that is, the developers—approach the funding of these projects relatively blind; no-one tells them why it's worth doing, and they haven't time to find out. So they bracket the work with site clearance and assume that it is being done to a minimum standard at minimum cost. Development control officers have tried to persuade developers to privilege research in their mitigation plans. They have also, by clever designs of their own, tried to persuade them to avoid the archaeology altogether. The way forward was shown by Ove Arup in 1991, who proposed a system of building on thin piles to minimize impact on the archaeological strata: even if archaeological investigation had still to take place on a comprehensive scale, it could be done by piling first and then excavating archaeologically between the piles. The developer could therefore put up the building and draw revenue from it without waiting for the archaeology to finish: the archaeological investigation could take its time and the developer could afford to pay for it. There are some reservations about this scheme, particularly in the matter of waterlogged deposits, which tend to rot as soon as the seal is broken and the air admitted (which is a consequence of piling). But maybe this is also a technical problem awaiting its solution.

In general, our clientele is still encouraged to just purge the whole of a site of its archaeology, and the profession's response is to standardize their procedures and to tick the boxes. It works because, as I suggested earlier, the client can't tell the difference between good and bad archaeology, only between the cheap and expensive, the quick and the lengthy. Much will depend on whether the client can be persuaded or obliged to accept archaeological intervention as a research opportunity rather than as site clearance. This will require the re-design of the tender package as a program of research and conservation, and a reconfiguration of the benefits to the sponsor in taxation and public support. As argued in Chapter 3, I believe this could happen because it would reflect a convergence with what is required of our discipline by the general public. If such a magic transformation could be effected, it would mean that space would be made in the CRM itinerary so that project design here has the same purpose and the same status as it does in academic research. Some ways in which this might be achieved are discussed in Chapter 6.

## INTEGRATED PROCUREMENT

Archaeological investigation is a creative activity for inventive people; that is my contention. Every project, however small, is a challenge to our curiosity and our intellect. For us, the basic factors powering what we do in the field are what we want to know—the objectives; what we can see—the terrain; and the community's attitude to our proposals, the social context. These things are assessed by evaluation and woven together in a design. It is in the creative act of design, I argue, rather than in dogmatic responses—those inherited or asserted rituals and traditions—that archaeology's truly original contribution can be seen by the rest of society. And when it is, the status of our subject in the commercial sector will rise.

Design is the motor that drives an archaeological project from an idea to an outcome, and in every project design we expect to see two programs: a program of research and a program of conservation. If this is accepted, it will be apparent that the greater part of current archaeological work does not qualify as research, whether done by academics or professionals. That is because it has no design. To fly over the countryside seeing what there is to see is reconnaissance; but so is digging random test pits, or rescue excavation, or even long-term excavation in which the project design is not published in advance. These can only be classed as reconnaissance too. Likewise, every evaluation that does not draw up a research agenda or study the social context, but confines itself only to the deposit model (as most do), is really only offering a reconnaissance of the site, not an assessment of its value.

For a project to achieve research status in the 21st century, it must not only have a project design (PD) with research and conservation programs, but that design must be widely publicized before it starts. Otherwise it cannot be claimed that stakeholders were consulted. In the case of commercial archaeology, this means that the PD must be lodged with the building plans for public inspection: this will help to break up the closed-door, underpriced stitch-ups between the developer, the curator, the consultant, and the contractor. In the case of academic projects, not only must the PD be published, but there is a strong case for the project requiring planning permission too. This will help to prevent private deals between governments, owners, and invited or self-invited research teams, and open up the research to design competition.

For larger projects, at least, the design competition should be conducted in public and subject to public comment, for both research and mitigation projects. As in the selection of an artist or an architect, detailed proposals should be drawn up and circulated and a panel or a plebiscite asked to choose from a short list. The selected archaeologist would then be invited to negotiate the budget. I need hardly emphasize that this hardly ever happens; to be frank, I know of no case other than Sutton Hoo where it has happened in the

143

research sector, and none at all in the commercial sector. The usual way archaeology happens is for an archaeologist to have an idea or see a disaster and then try to raise the money to do some work; or for a developer to invite a contractor selected from a consultants' list to get the archaeology out of the way, often on the basis of the lowest price.

What I am proposing now is a system much closer to architecture than site clearance. In the commercial sector, we can bring a special product to the design meeting—an ancestry for every new building. If we can convince our clients that that is what they are paying for, everything else follows: the research dividend is increased, the status of the contractors is increased, and the cultural heritage of the nation is genuinely enriched. My vision for the profession thus has us working in small partnerships in white coats, designing imaginative responses to research opportunities. We would be technically adroit—invasive but not destructive, fielding the latest scientific methods of investigation at a distance. We would expect the engineering designers to respond in similar vein, by putting their buildings on stilts and rafts, to conserve whatever we don't need to dissect. The matching of the archaeological and the engineering design represents the overall heritage cost of the project. Its price will be determined by the developer's anticipated profit and by the value of the research dividend to the project as a whole. On the archaeological side, this will mean larger fees shared by fewer, more expert, people. I don't think this is fantasy.

On the other hand, a larger, more active group of avocational participants is also an integral part of the vision. Students and volunteers take virtually no part in commercial archaeology, and yet the commercial old guard, who do not provide for their presence, also moan about how untrained they are. It seems to me logical and useful that student apprentices and the local archaeological society volunteers should be part of any commercial project design. These poor creatures are practically extinct, deprived of their grazing by the professional dinosaurs. And yet they are our popular base, founts of local knowledge and local support. In other words, a commercial design that has the local archaeological society as participants in it should be assessed as having added value over one that doesn't.

But the most important link to forge is that between the commercial sector and the universities, a link conspicuous by its absence both on the ground and in the British, American, Swedish, and Irish statements on the historic environment we looked at in Chapter 3. The nature of archaeological design is that it requires a research program and a conservation program to be delivered in a social context. This is always true, whether the principal driver is a university, a commercial outfit, or a member of an archaeological society. The logical way to make this come true is to ensure that the three parties—the universities, the commercial companies, and the archaeological societies—work together in every project (FIG. 5.5). Projects that are mainly research will be led by universities, but should employ professional companies to do the fieldwork at commercial rates—because fieldwork is an expertise that most university lecturers don't have. Projects that are mainly mitigation will be led by the commercial sector and should employ university lecturers and integrate their knowledge into the design process, because that is expertise the company staff don't have. Both need the local archaeological society, among others, as a convenient way of ensuring that the key factors of local archaeological knowledge and the social context are fed into their designs.

If this happens, the academic and the commercial sectors will no longer be separated and moribund. The two strands of our business will have joined up in one living, breathing, kicking organism.

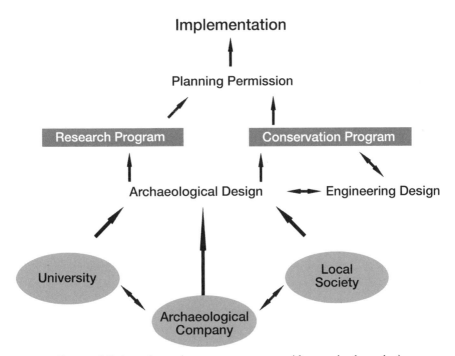

FIGURE 5.5. An enhanced procurement system (*diagram by the author*).

# CHAPTER 6

# MAKING ARCHAEOLOGY

# HAPPEN

## SCOTTISH PRELUDE

One place that we haven't visited as yet is Scotland, which is odd since it is my home country, insofar as I have one: most members of my family were born there or have married Scots (like salmon, we return to mate). Archaeologically, it provides a good example of a well-integrated, well-managed small country. And yet . . . .

Scotland is the north end of the island of Britain and has a truly stunning variety of terrain: a central massif (the Grampians) cut to the east by long estuaries and inlets (the Firthlands) and broken up in the north and west into chains of islands. In the south and east are rich extents of arable pasture. Geographically, if you turn Scotland upside down, it occupies a similar position in the North Sea as Greece does in the eastern Mediterranean, a central place in a busy maritime world. Prehistoric peoples settled in three different zones around the mountains in the center, each looking out toward a different country: the east to Scandinavia, the west to Ireland, and the south to England. In the first millennium AD, the east was occupied by the Picts (Britons), the west by the Scots (Irish), and the south by the English, with the Norse settling in much of the northern and western isles. The history and archaeology of the Scottish peninsula is intimately connected to other places across land and sea.

In spite of its heterogeneous origins and maritime location, Scotland has long campaigned on a nationalist agenda—which may one day result in independence. Research objectives also tend toward a national narrative, and heritage regulation toward national needs. In some ways this is productive: the grandly named Royal Commission of Ancient and Historical Monuments is probably the best archaeological survey team on the planet. In other ways, it is inappropriate: in prehistoric and early historic times, identity was focused not on a central rocky landmass, but on patches of water with land on either side; in other words, the most interesting archaeological questions involve the neighboring countries—which now have different languages and legislation.

As well as the more familiar repertoire of flat sites and towns, Scotland has some regional specialties: cairns, castles, crannogs, and bogs, and has developed exemplary ways of dealing with them. Cairns are heaps of stone with little soil, usually covering a burial of the Bronze Age. They have to be taken apart stone by stone and viewed from high up to see the phases (FIG. 6.1; Mercer and Midgley 1997). The castles are picturesque piles of the medieval period and

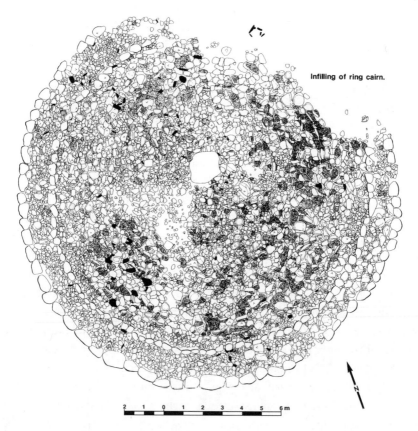

Infilling of ring cairn.

FIGURE 6.1. Excavation of a stone cairn at Sketewan (Mercer and Midgley 1997, 300; courtesy of the Society of Antiquaries of Scotland).

later (FIG. 6.2), and tourists are attracted by their aura of dramatic conflict. Archaeological projects may involve surveying, digging, recording wall fabric, and rummaging in archives—with a view to investigating the whole sequence of the castle and its predecessors, conserving the extant ruin and designing public visits (e.g., FAS-Heritage 2010). Crannogs are artificial islands in lochs, of the Iron Age and later. They usually had one small wooden building on them and a timber causeway that provided access from the bank. An example in Loch Tay, Oakbank, was completely excavated underwater, the divers hovering over a delicate murky deposit of soft timbers, seeds, leaves, fruit, sheep droppings, and timber piles, all wonderfully preserved. It has since been reconstructed in situ with new timbers (Dixon 2004). In a 2005 wetland survey, which listed 353 crannogs, Anne Crone and Ciara Clarke also drew attention to the Scottish bogs which account for 72% of British peat, the Flow Country of the northeast being one of the largest surviving intact blanket bogs.

Such raised wetland is notoriously hard to dig, especially if occupied by prehistoric people with a very sparse material culture. Rod McCullagh and Richard Tipping had the task of mapping a corridor 3.5 km long and 300 m

FIGURE 6.2. Girnigoe Castle, Sutherland, undergoing a program of investigation, restoration, conservation, and display (*FAS Heritage Ltd*).

149

wide through such country in Sutherland—the now classic survey of Achany Glen (FIG. 6.3a; McCullagh and Tipping 1998). In a reconnaissance phase, they divided their corridor into 50 × 50 m blocks, each examined by surface inspection in transects spaced at 5 m intervals. As a result, 752 features were recognized in 237 blocks, although 13% of these were later rejected as being natural humps and hollows. Detailed topography and vegetation boundaries were also recorded, together with samples of soil depth. This stage was completed by 16 fieldworkers in 22 weeks. In the evaluation stage, 30% of the sites already located were selected randomly and visited by a field team who cut a 2 × 1 m trench through each one. The soil profiles and pedology were recorded and sampled in each trench, using survey, drawing, and video footage. Significance (relative value) was then ascribed to every 50 m block using a formula based on rarity, quality, and clustering of features, and the results used to compile a *significance map* presented in the form of contours (FIG. 6.3b). A mitigation project was then designed. On the management side, zones of low significance were deemed to indicate a good route for the new road. On the research side, sites were selected for area excavation in zones of high significance, especially where they had exhibited a wide range of dates (to give sequence) or a broad spatial distribution (to show use of space). Making visual records was affected by variability of color and texture due to changing light and humidity, so every excavated context was also represented by a 10 liter bulk sample, of which 0.5 liter was extracted as a soil sample, the remainder wet-screened (0.355 mm mesh) and the flot and retent hand-sorted. The constituents so extracted formed the definition of the content of the context. Twenty-seven sites were excavated, 4,000 soil samples were processed, and 80 specimens submitted to micromorphology. The eventual yield from the project included a detailed environmental history and descriptions of an early Bronze cairn, Bronze Age round houses and clearance cairns, an Iron Age defended site, numerous field boundaries, and a late 18th-century long house. The publication of the project included a client report, scholarly publication, and presentations to the citizens of the Lairg district. In a poignant example of public affection toward our profession, one of the younger members of the local community offered the team a telling assessment in writing (FIG. 6.4).

This fine project serves for dozens of others, undertaken by commercial firms through the good offices of the state agency, Historic Scotland, using the local planning regulation NPPG5. In their 2004 review, Bradley and Phillips praised Scotland's response to developer-funded opportunities and showed

a

b

FIGURE 6.3. (*a*) Achany Glen, Scotland (McCullagh and Tipping 1998; *courtesy of Rod McCullagh
and Historic Scotland*); (*b*) its significance map
prior to road widening (McCullagh and Tipping
1998; *courtesy of Rod McCullagh and Historic
Scotland*).

how it had revealed parts of prehistory that research might never have
reached, if left to researchers. The coverage was naturally uneven and, in fact,
non-random since most development was in the lowland zones. But the result
of digging large numbers of settlements, cemeteries, and field systems (as
opposed to monuments) not only put ordinary sites into balance with the

151

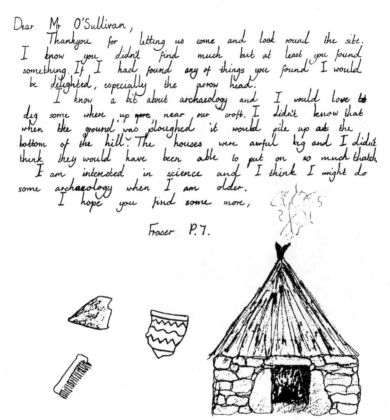

FIGURE 6.4. Achany Glen; facsimile of a letter of appreciation from Fraser, a year 7 visitor from Rogart School. The text reads: *Dear Mr O'Sullivan, Thank you for letting us come and look round the site. I know you didn't find much but at least you found something. If I had found any of things you found I would have been delighted, especially the arrowhead. I know a bit about archaeology and I would love to dig somewhere, up near our croft. I didn't know that when the ground was ploughed it would pile up at the bottom of the hill. The houses were awful big and I didn't think they would have been able to put on as much thatch. I am interested in science and I think I might do some archaeology when I am older. I hope you find some more* (McCullagh and Tipping 1998; reproduced by kind permission of Rod McCullagh and Historic Scotland).

extraordinary ones, it also radically altered the agenda. "For the first time," says Bradley, "the pace of fieldwork may have outstripped that of current research, as it has in every part of Britain and Ireland" (Phillips and Bradley 2004, 44).

The funding for these projects comes from a multitude of sources: the developers, the state agency Historic Scotland, clan chiefs and private owners of castles, the Heritage Lottery fund, local authorities, and a number of Trust funds and learned societies. This shows a healthy interest in the subject by many of its citizens. But, surprisingly, Scotland has had less success in associating archaeology with the national identity than its neighbors. There is an obsession with England, Bonnie Prince Charlie, and whisky, while the magnificence of the prehistoric monuments is largely ignored in tourist literature. Compare Denmark, where the popular Danish-language archaeology magazine *Skalk* has a distribution of over 17,000 and there is massive investment in prehistoric sites such as Jelling and Lejhre. In Scotland, archaeological tourism should be of comparable importance—and for good economic reasons. In his MA dissertation of 2008, Paul Burtenshaw calculated the overall use-value to the economy of the Kilmartin site at £5 million per year. This is an attraction based overwhelmingly on people wishing to see a group of prehistoric monuments—and not just to see them, but to know their story. If this is the case at a place that has seen no recent high-profile field research, one can imagine the potential attraction if it got the same treatment as Lejhre, Carnac, or Stonehenge.

In the matter of archaeology, Scotland is coy about research as well as tourism. Ireland, its neighbor to the west, has a centrally funded Discovery Programme dedicated to the establishment of a national prehistoric story through archaeology (*www.discoveryprogramme.ie/*). But in spite of its nationalist agenda, Scotland has no comparable national research facility. The attitude toward investigation for research purposes is rigid rather than critical, with the result that famous sites like Iona have been nibbled to death by tiny trenches (J. O'Sullivan 1999). The recently issued *Scottish Heritage Environment Policy* (SHEP) hardly mentions research at all, and when it does, implies that it is something extra required by the academic community that conservationists must reluctantly cater to: "Scottish ministers believe that there needs to be greater awareness, knowledge and understanding of the historic environment. This needs to address lay, vocational, technical, professional, scientific and academic needs" (Historic Scotland 2009). It is, of course, the public (and the politicians) that need the research, and the academics who do it on their behalf, not the other way round. But eerily, in a list of fourteen partners in this vision for the "knowledge and understanding" of Scotland's Historic Environment, the universities are not mentioned.

A last anecdote emphasizes the sad status of research in today's normal mitigation procedures. In a recent planning application to erect a wind farm on the northeast coast, I was on one side attempting to defend the integrity of a piece of historic environment, and an archaeological company was on the other, commissioned to evaluate the impact of the construction. The company, as a viable business, was obliged to do only what was required of it by the local authority and the national advisors (which was not very much), since this determined the amount of money the client (the wind-farm builder) was obliged to pay. And yet we know (cf. Chapter 2) that the archaeological value of a piece of land is determined not by routine prescriptions, or even by what appears to be on the ground, but by how hard you look. Thus all parties were operating in irons, and the archaeology itself had no voice. It was not mandatory to consult a local expert (me, in this case), since the objective was to minimize the archaeology, not to enhance it. By some strange contortion, the archaeological contractor was being retained by the client to assess the impact of the archaeology on the development project, rather than the other way about.

And yet, everyone who has decided to do archaeology for a living starts by championing the value and excitement of the material past, and should be allowed to go on championing its assets without having the enthusiasm crushed out of them by dogmatic regulations or procedures. The commercial sector employs some of the best archaeologists of their generation, and the aim of the profession should be to liberate their creativity, not by claiming that everything they do is research—it plainly isn't—but through the competitive exercise of design.

## DEFINING THE PRODUCT

This Scottish prelude encapsulates the dilemma of deregulated countries and returns us to the central questions of these essays: why is our discipline so disjointed and undervalued, and what is to be done about it? Research, conservation, and display are all part of the same mission, and universities, the state, archaeological firms, and consultants are all in the same line of business. It is a huge business, but its several components hardly even give lip-service to the nuclear force that holds it together—finding out about the past. The task that lies before us is to invent a way of making archaeology happen in a manner that is ethically aligned, financially viable, and intellectually satisfying. One way of doing this is to define a common product for all branches of archaeology and all its sponsors and clients. That product is new knowledge.

I am aware that I write about a problem that not everyone believes they have. Tom King shows that, although archaeological investigation is not mandatory under Section 106, it usually happens (2005, 37) and it is widely accepted to be research (King 2005, 29). Indeed, prolonged involvement in impact management (mitigation) is held to offer a career in research: "It's not unusual to find people . . . —smart, talented hard-working—who have developed stable, reasonably well-paying jobs doing productive research in the context of CRM" (King 2005, 102). One would certainly like this to be true, and if it is, for the United States to share its secret with every other country. The impression persists, however, that even in America, there is a canyon between the academic and commercial sectors, or at least between what each regards as research. Which is not to deny that it's a canyon that intrepid people will cross.

Every business needs a product, preferably one that other people want. In archaeology's struggle to define the essence of its social and financial value, there is a natural tendency to make ourselves all-encompassing, not only capable of unearthing the past, but predicting the future, helping the poor, and righting wrongs. A modern archaeology, according to Jeremy Sabloff (2008), can inform and inspire society on subjects like climate change, sustainability, warfare, and urban life. This is certainly the case, and one could add others, such as the urge to spread our genes, organize other people, and cheat fear through spirituality and ritual. If our value lies in our relevance, Sabloff believes we can demonstrate it through what he calls "action archaeology"—going out and restoring ancient irrigation systems or traditional housing. I would not argue with that either, but it may be that such opportunities are neither widespread nor welcome. The call to use archaeology to improve people's lives in the present and plan for a better future is admirable and may command consensus, but sponsors might rather give some of their profits to a proper NGO and get tax relief for it.

On the other hand, I am convinced that no post-colonial inhibitions should prevent us from importing archaeology itself, as a universal science, into other countries. It seems to me only logical that an overseas aid package should include funds that help a country rediscover its own past—but only that. The truth is that what many people most want from archaeology we can't (or won't) give them: large amounts of kudos and money from digging up safe sites or treasure, evidence that their particular ethnic group has an ancestral right to occupy a territory, proof that Atlantis was real, god exists, the Bible is true, and so on. We can only give people what we know and, like explorers, let our pictures, our convictions, and our theories speak for us, as clearly as possible.

It is often suggested that the successful marketing of archaeology depends not on the product itself, but on the energy with which it is promoted. The number-one favorite strategy for raising our profile is to improve communication with the public, and we are failing in this because academics are inhibited by their research competitors from getting into popular writing or television; or if they do, they get castigated for it by their peers and lose credibility (Sabloff 2008, 106–107). But we should also face the fact that not everyone knows how to write for the public, and that doesn't make them bad archaeologists. We have many excellent researchers, scholars, and excavators who have no wish to expose their inner child or become media tarts. Those who urge scholars to communicate with the public have their heart in the right place; but those who actually do it know that it is not a hobby for the summer holidays, but a full-time job for a tyrannical master. Television, for example, requires the eager archaeologist to suffer capricious contracts, endless inconsequential meetings, interminable hours on the telephone, relentless travel, and a huge wastage rate of footage, cut by directors who are incontinent with their praise but blithely ignore the archaeological message, since they remain ultimately convinced of their superior sense of what the public really wants. Which is all that matters. Writing for a popular audience is not a spare-time occupation either; you have agents and publishers who always know better than you do, and as soon as there is a prospect of success, you are off to nocturnal signings in the bookshops of obscure towns or their weird festivals. In brief, you become their creature; they don't publish you because they love your work, but because you make them money. I am not saying this is a lesser life than doing archaeology; it just isn't the same one, and these days it can't be done on the side. There are excellent journalists, producers, and popular writers—they just need feeding.

As an alternative, it might be worth promoting the following unfashionable idea: that archaeologists should begin by serving science. It seems to me that the priority in the process of getting our work widely appreciated is to make sure that it is intelligible to others. This is why the journal *Antiquity* exists, and at a more basic level, why we write textbooks. Every issue of

*Antiquity* results in three or four articles in the newspapers in England, the United States, and especially Germany. Every textbook written for a student is also written for a parent. They expect it to be serious, rather than sexy. In other words, archaeologists have two dedicated public sectors already: for the academics their students, for the commercial profession their developers. These are more than just elements of the public, they are clients, and we have plenty of incentive for improving communication with them (King 2005, 106).

The media like to sell archaeology as the rapture of explorers and the disagreement of experts; the mitigation industry sells archaeology as an exercise in efficient elimination. But these are not our real products. Our real product is not the doing of archaeology or the avoiding of it, but the winning of new information about the past. Whether in the bookshop or the boardroom, our sponsors are buying knowledge, and we must keep them focused on that. To try to disguise our true product in a colorful or virtuous wrapping is unnecessary and even risky. Knowledge is a recognized commodity and has its own market value; it is our task to sell it. What are we afraid of?

## Ways of Working

My previous essays raised some of the obstacles to this mission: the splitting of the profession into its academic, administrative, and commercial sectors; the present tendency for each sector to embrace just one part of the agenda—for the academics, teaching and research; for the administrators, conservation of landscapes and monuments; for the commercial sector, mitigation or impact management. Crossovers are desired and sometimes claimed, but hard to achieve in practice. I asserted that all aspects of the mission come together in the practice of archaeological investigation in which sites are defined, given a value, studied and published in a staged procedure powered by design (Chapter 5). We are therefore looking to define an integrated system of procurement, in which universities, commercial firms, and local enthusiasts collaborate in creating designs that make the maximum research use of development opportunities.

Several times I have made sly comparisons with architects, betraying a belief that a firm of architects represents a suitable model for us, one that is naturally in partnership with builders, but operates in a slightly different way. There are parallels to be found in the architect's profession that might be helpful in reconstructing our own. The American Institute of Architecture, for example, is clear that clients view design as the core competency of architects.

In dealing with these clients, architects are encouraged to cultivate and foster relationships, demonstrate flexibility and proficiency in design, become master communicators, emphasize specialized skills and knowledge, strengthen business skills, and educate the client. At the base of the business strategy is "the firm's collective knowledge. That is what clients pay for, and a design firm must be structured as a learning organization." A response to a Request for Qualifications—that is, "reasons why you should hire us"—contains not only the scope of work, design, Gantt chart, and other devices that archaeologists will be familiar with, but "a general statement of the firm's approach with particular focus on distinguishing characteristics or services." Included is a description of the actual staff members who will be on site, with a mention of their previous projects and interests. This goes a long way past the average archaeological tender, because it is a service that is not being sold on price and default practice, but on the benefits of a creative approach and the original thinking of a firm's personalities. It is easy to see at a glance why architects are better paid than archaeologists: they value their own contributions more highly (*http://www.aia.org/aiaucmp/groups/ek_members/documents*).

Drawing on the same source, it is also perhaps worth listening to the more senior profession on the subject of future viability: "It makes sense to be uneasy about what's coming around the bend, despite the current robust marketplace, evidenced by many firms having more work than they say they can handle—yet taking on additional projects anyway. Further evidence is the extreme difficulties some firms are encountering in their efforts to find and recruit talent, compounded by competitors' efforts to recruit away people already in place." The unease is attributed to a number of factors, including expected downturns, intrusion of non-traditional providers into the marketplace, and anxieties about the competence of the next generation of practitioners. In response, they urge firms not to cut fees, but to price services on the basis of value provided, to avoid working with clients who are unwilling to pay for the value of the results (and let them know why), and to serve clients well. They promote the "seven attributes of design-first firms" as:

- Foster an entrepreneurial culture.

- Develop strategic plans.

- Plan leadership succession.

- Motivate talent.

- Use an integrated design process.

- Promote sustainable design.

- Encourage a learning environment.

This kind of collegiate encouragement can also be found in some archaeological professional bodies (e.g., ACRA, p. 81), but we seem to lack the level of self-confidence, the feeling of being wanted and necessary. The entertaining posting "My client doesn't understand me" features this observation from a user: "[Our firm] combines a sustained belief in the power of design with real-world understanding of the business objectives of our clients" (*http://www.justpractising.com/its-about-money-stupidarchitects-my-client-doesn't-understand-me/#comments*). This seems to me a valid strapline for the consultant archaeologist too. Within the architect's design lies the concept of a new building; within the archaeological design lies a different product, but one that's more permanent and will be appreciated for longer and more widely: new knowledge. We have every reason to promote it for what it is. On this interpretation, the commercial archaeology company is still a business, but it is a business employed for its expertise before its efficiency: it puts learning first.

## A Tentative Scheme

Walking the tightrope between finding a useful business analogy and knowing that it's different, I offer a sketch here of a way that archaeology might work in a deregulated society in future years. Let's assume that the argument for the primacy of design has been won, that the profession desires, for the sake of its product, to move away from the old dogmas and release the inventive and creative energies that we have noted in so many exemplary projects. It is this invention and creativity, I have endeavored to argue, that will eventually raise the public value of what we do. That is not to say that "default systems" don't have their uses; but they should serve design rather than having design serve them.

If design is the driver and the nugget of an archaeological project, then it follows that contracts should be awarded on the merits of design, not on the lowest offered price. The process of design competition invites applications in outline, followed by a second invitation directed to a selected short list to work up a fuller program and detail the outcomes. Ideally this latter stage should include evaluation, so that the candidates may know something of the terrain and social context they will be dealing with, without having to lay out large

159

amounts of money themselves. Design competition of a kind does occasionally take place already, but it would be naive to pretend that it is the research dividend, rather than the cost, that is determinant.

Since most archaeological investigation is now undertaken at the expense of developers, it is important to consider why they would want to embrace such a system. In the first place, it would do no harm to redraft or enhance a government's planning guidance so as to emphasize that the social purpose of mitigation is to maximize a research opportunity, not to preserve an imaginary monument (by recording it). However, a developer and his shareholders will still need to be convinced that the newly defined product is not only worth paying for, but will not necessarily result in paying more. The consequence of adopting design competition (as opposed to competitive tender) is that the cost of archaeology may increase. I say "may" because a design that targets particular historical problems and uses the new techniques of nano-archaeology may actually move less earth and therefore cost less, than the blanket "total excavation." The first part of the argument could be straightforward: developers are educated people and, in my experience at least, are more sympathetic to the notion that they are offering a research opportunity for the general benefit, rather than giving the site over to archaeologists because the government says they must. There are also altruistic rewards to be gained from publicity won by the discoveries.

However, the fact that a research opportunity gives public benefit ought also to attract some official compensation—for example, tax advantages for those facilitating it. A good design, with overt research objectives stated in advance, should also be eligible for research grants and public asset grants (e.g., Heritage Lottery). Such a protocol could be brought into being tomorrow, if the local and central authorities allowed it. It would hardly need a law or even a new regulation, since it is in keeping with those that already exist and arguably reflects that spirit more exactly. None of it is a million miles from what is already practiced, occasionally or in part—but public acceptance of such a method of procurement would deliver better archaeology and a more integrated, purposeful profession.

Is the profession ready? At present, the research and mitigation procurement systems follow separate itineraries. In Britain, neither the academic nor the commercial sector is competent, on its own, to bid for a large archaeological project by design competition. The universities don't have the management or technical skills, and the companies don't have the knowledge base. In some ways this is an excellent state of affairs, because it means that every design competition will oblige academics and professionals to get together in a common cause and prepare an integrated design, with strong research, management, conservation, and display.

It seems unlikely that all archaeological projects would be procured by design competition, any more than all architecture is. *De facto* or *de jure*, planners would set a threshold, in overall cost or overall area affected, above which design competition would be the norm. That leaves the plethora of small evaluation and other projects, which tend to benefit less from originality than from experience. As we have noticed along the way, there are advantages in archaeologists attaching themselves to a certain piece of geography, and several projects would not have happened at all without the persistence and insight of a local enthusiast or expert (e.g., p. 106). Bearing in mind that a great many archaeological projects warrant only very small-scale intervention, coupled with desktop or archive work undertaken for purposes of evaluation, there is a clear case for a firm specializing in a region, or even in a particular branch of archaeology: West Midlands Historic Buildings Inc. or Bronze Age Scotland Ltd.

This begins to generate a professional landscape not unlike architecture, in which a broad hierarchy of companies, large and small, develop local, regional, national, or international practices. Some of their contracts will be won by regional or national competitions, on the basis of research outcome, and their designs published in advance, as part of the planning proposal, for public scrutiny. Other contracts can be small-scale local interventions, prompted by routine refurbishment or emergency discoveries, work that results in a gradual piecemeal accumulation of local knowledge. All these contracts, whether huge and short-term or small and long-term, would need to be subject to peer-group quality control—something that commercial archaeology does not yet have. But quality control of what is actually done in the name of archaeology seems more appropriate to our line of business than a code of conduct or the compulsory use of a default practice.

There is one element of our community that we do have but architects don't, although I am sure they would like it, and that is our avocational following. There are hundreds of thousands of people who would love to contribute to archaeological research but are routinely excluded from it. They are often organized into local societies that meet regularly to exercise their interest. While television producers are fretting about the viewing figures of an archaeology program fronted by a celebrity, the dedicated public are out listening to a talk by a real archaeologist in a village hall, and asking their questions and having their say. And may it always be so. "Community archaeology" is an attempt to reach out the hand of friendship to this group through participation in a few projects with low health and safety risks. But we can do better. The participation of local unpaid enthusiasts in high-profile research and mitigation projects would not just be interesting for them; it would bring added value to the project by way of local knowledge of prehistory and modern empathy of place. I realize that the hazards of a building site are not readily compatible with the use of volunteers; I am talking rather about the background knowledge embedded in local archives and museums, which enriches research and engages the public. The prospect of such collaboration and its added value should be a winning aspect in a design competition.

FIGURE 5.5 showed in diagrammatic form how the archaeological community might work together to canalize the streams of developer funding into a river of research. Universities, governments, commercial firms, and avocational archaeologists are presently connected to each other by thousands of tiny threads, but no common working network. Each of these communities is imprisoned in its own black box, with little of that constant movement between them that seems to be such an attractive part of the scene in the United States (King 2005, 97–122) and so rare elsewhere. Even so, the working conditions of each métier are constrained by the regulations that govern them and determine what and how much they will be paid. This affects the way practitioners think about archaeology and how much of themselves they believe they can give to its true objectives.

## ENVOI

We have a fight on our hands of a kind that Wheeler, 50 years on, would have relished. We have won our share of society's flattery and cash, but lost our souls in the marketplace. In universities, the hard currency of research consists of ever greater generalization about the past, rather than its particularities, while economies of scale demand ever broader, shallower-taught degrees, in which archaeology risks becoming a module in some vague competence like "social science" and scurries to embrace sociological subjects like "heritage." Even where archaeology remains a discipline of its own, students are not taught about the archaeology of the world, our real theater, nor are they taught about the profession most of them will join. By an ironical contrast, the one thing they excel in—ways of interpreting material culture through a variety of paradigms—appears to have little use in a commercial firm.

In the commercial world, the hard currency is profit, and the emphasis first and last is on business. Members of firms themselves might fret about their academic status, but are obliged to use their own efficiency, rather than the research dividends they have won, as their main marketing tool. An archaeological firm flourishes by acquiring others, becoming "a bigger and bigger operation with more and more contracts" (King 2005, 103). Meanwhile, the legislators that license them find that more and more of the redundant material world comes under the heading of "heritage," resulting in the increasing costs of keeping minor ruins standing, and sterilizing land that could be researched, or built on, or both. The avocational archaeologist, backbone of the subject, is a backbone growing soft through underuse. By contrast, treasure hunters—in England, at any rate—are publicly congratulated and rewarded at the market rate for anything they find, often amounting to millions of pounds, while museums are starved of funds. The presentation of archaeology in the media is emerging as practically a profession of its own, conducted by full-time publicists who can present anything from archaeology to politics to gardening and sometimes seem confused between them. It might seem that that the subject as a whole is suffering from a kind of heritage inflation.

Beneath all this flummery, we actually live in a golden age for research. Archaeological investigation can potentially see more, sense more, understand more, than ever it could before. All over the world people are doing archaeology in new and interesting ways and finding new and interesting things. Our passion for storytelling has increased by leaps and bounds, and our enthusiasm for grand narratives continually enlarges. We are demonstrating that the long, strange, noble, ignoble, human experience on the planet is of concern to everyone. We have sturdy procedures for investigation in the field, and may slowly emerge from our dependence on default systems to become a more vivacious and inventive profession. We have a potentially dedicated public, who love what we do, are impatient with media condescension, and will pay to conserve deposits and structures, the materials of our research, at local, national, and international levels.

All of this great enterprise is driven by one thing: wanting to know more and understand more about the past. This is our purpose and our product. Society does not value us because we know how to make money out of them, nor because we can think of fifteen ways of interpreting the Neolithic, but because we will find out what happened on the planet and add it to the sum of human knowledge. As is already widely appreciated, this is a type of knowledge with enormous practical and spiritual implications. It will be worth brandishing the mission and holding on tight to its objectives ourselves. Generating new understanding of the human experience is what we do, what we are good at, what we are paid for, and, ultimately, is what will make archaeology continue to happen.

# REFERENCES

Ammann, Brigitta, Alex R. Furger, Marcel Joos, and Helga Liese-Kleiber. 1977. *Der bronzezeitliche Einbaum und die nachneolithischen Sedimente*. Die neolithischen Ufersiedlungen von Twann, Band 3. Bern: Staatlicher Lehrmittleverlag.

Andrews G., J. Barrett, and J. Lewis. 2000. Interpretation not record: The practice of archaeology. *Antiquity* 74: 525–530.

Andrews, G., and R. Thomas 1995. The management of archaeological projects: Theory and practice in the UK. In Malcolm Cooper, Anthony Firth, John Carman, and David Wheatley (eds.), *Managing Archaeology*, 189–207. London: Routledge.

Arup, Ove, and partners and University of York. 1991. *York Development and Archaeology Study*. English Heritage.

Aston, M. A., M. H. Martin, and A. W. Jackson. 1998. The potential for heavy soil analysis on low status archaeological sites at Shapwick, Somerset. *Antiquity* 72: 838–847.

Balkansky, Andrew K., Stephen A. Kowalewski, Veronica Perez Rodriguez, Thomas J. Pluckhahn, Charlotte A. Smith, Laura R. Stiver, Dmitri Beliaev, John F. Chamblee, Verenice Y. Heredia Espinoza, and Roberto Santos Perez. 2000. Archaeological survey in the Mixteca Alta of Oaxaca, Mexico. *Journal of Field Archaeology*, 27.4: 365–389.

Barker, P. A. 1977. *Techniques of Archaeological Excavation*. London: Batsford.

Becker H. 2008. Caesium magnetometry for landscape archaeology. In S. Campana and S. Piro (eds.), *Seeing the Unseen—Geophysics and Landscape Archaeology*, 129–166. CRC Press.

Berggren A., and I. Hodder. 2003, Social practice, method, and some problems of field archaeology. *American Antiquity* 68.3: 421–434.

Binford, Lewis R. 1964. A consideration of archaeological research design. *American Antiquity* 29: 425–441.

——. 1972. *An Archaeological Perspective*. Seminar Press.

——. 2001. Where do research problems come from? *American Antiquity* 66.4: 669–678.

——. 2007. Epilogue. In James M. Skibo, Michael W. Graves, and Miriam T. Stark (eds.), *Archaeological Anthropology. Perspectives on Method and Theory*, 236–242. Tucson: University of Arizona Press.

Black, Stephen L., and Kevin Jolly. 2003. *Archaeology by Design*. Archaeologists Toolkit 1. Walnut Creek, CA: AltaMira.

Blakey Michael L. 2001. Bioachaeology of the African diaspora in the Americas: Its origin and scope. *Annual Review of Anthropology* 30: 387–422.

Bland, Roger. 2005. A pragmatic approach to the problem of portable antiquities: The experience of England and Wales. *Antiquity* 79: 440–447.

Bostyn, Françoise. 2004. *Néolithique ancien en Normandie: Le Village Villeneuve-Saint-Germain de Poses "Sur la Mare" et les sites de la bouche du Vaudreuil*. La Société Préhistorique Française/INRAP.

Bowkett, L., S. Hill, Diana and K. A. Wardle. 2009. *Classical Archaeology in the Field: Approaches*. Bristol Classical Press.

Brothwell, D. R., and A. M. Pollard (eds.). 2001. *Handbook of Archaeological Sciences*. John Wiley and Sons.

Brown, T. A. 2001 Ancient DNA. In Brothwell and Pollard 2001, 301–312.

Buckley, Michael, Matthew Collins, Jane Thomas-Oates, and Julie C. Wilson. 2009. Species identification by analysis of bone collagen using matrix-assisted laser desorption/ionisation time-of-flight mass spectrometry. *Rapid Communications in Mass Spectrometry* 23: 3843–3854.

Burger,Oskar, Lawrence C. Todd, Paul Burnett, Tomas J. Stohlgren, and Doug Stephens. 2004. Multi-scale and nested-intensity sampling techniques for archaeological survey. *Journal of Field Archaeology* 29.3/4 (Autumn 2002–Winter 2004): 409–423.

Burnouf, Joelle, Jean-Oliver Guilhot, Marie-Odile Mandy, and Christian Orcel. 1991. *Le Pont de la Guilotière. Franchir le Rhône a Lyon*. Lyon: Circonscriptions des Antiquités Historiques.

Burrow, Ian. 2010. Review of Paul Everill's *The Invisible Diggers. Antiquity* 84: 256.

Burtenshaw, Paul. 2008. Archaeology, economics and tourism: The economic use-value of archaeology with the case study of Kilmartin Glen and Kilmartin House Museum. Unpublished MA dissertation, University College London.

Carman, John. 2004. Excavating excavation: A contribution to the social archaeology of archaeology. In Geoff Carver (ed.), *Digging the Dirt. Excavation in the New Millennium*, 47–51. BAR International series 1256.

Carver, Martin. 1979. Three Saxo-Norman tenements in Durham City. *Medieval Archaeology* 23: 1–80.

——. 1983. Forty French towns: An essay on archaeological site evaluation and historical aims. *Oxford Journal of Archaeology* 2.3: 339–378.

——. 1993. *Arguments in Stone: Archaeological Research and the European Town in the First Millennium AD* (being the Dalrymple Lectures for 1990). Oxford: Oxbow and University of Glasgow.

——. 1996. On archaeological value. *Antiquity* 70: 45–56.

——. 2001. The future of field archaeology. In Z. Kobylinski (ed.), *Quo vadis archaeologia? Whither European Archaeology in the 21st Century*, 118–132. Warsaw: European Science Foundation.

——. 2002. Marriages of true minds: Archaeology with texts. In B. Cunliffe, W. Davies, and C. Renfrew (eds.), *Archaeology: The Widening Debate*, 465–496. British Academy.

——. 2003. *Archaeological Value and Evaluation*. Mantua: Società Archeologica Padana.

——. 2005. *Sutton Hoo. A Seventh-Century Princely Burial Ground and Its Context*. British Museum Publications.

——. 2008. *Portmahomack Monastery of the Picts*. Edinburgh University Press.

——. 2009. *Archaeological Investigation*. London and New York: Routledge.

Carver, Martin, and Djemal Souidi. 1996. Archaeological reconnaissance and evaluation in the Achir Basin (Algeria). *Archéologie islamique* 6: 7–44.

Carver, Martin, and Cecily Spall. 2004. Excavating a *parchmenerie*: Archaeological correlates of making parchment at the Pictish monastery at Portmahomack, Easter Ross. *Proceedings of the Society of Antiquaries of Scotland* 134: 183–200.

Carver, M., S. Donaghey, and A. B. Sumpter. 1978. Riverside structures and a well in Skeldergate and buildings in Bishophill. *The Archaeology of York* 4.1. London: Council for British Archaeology.

Cassen, Serge. 2009. Autour de la Table. *Explorations archéologiques et discours savants sur des architectures néolithiques a Locmariaquer, Morhiban (Table des Marchands et Grand Menhir)*. CNRS et Université de Nantes.

Catteddu, Isabelle. 2009. *Archéologie médiévale en France: Le premier Moyen Âge (Ve–XIe siècle)*. Paris: La Découverte.

CEEQUAL. 2008. The Civil Engineering Environmental Quality and Awards Scheme. Retrieved from *www.ceequal.com*.

Challis, K., A. J. Howard, M. Kincey, and C. J. Carey. 2008. Analysis of the Effectiveness of Airborne Lidar Backscattered Laser Intensity for Predicting Organic Preservation Potential of Waterlogged Deposits. Retrieved from *http://ads.ahds.ac.uk/catalogue/resources.html?lidar_eh_2008*.

Chester-Kaldwell, Mary E. 2008. Early Anglo-Saxon communities in the landscape of Norfolk: Cemeteries and metal-detector finds in context. Unpublished PhD dissertation, University of Cambridge.

China, State Administration of Cultural Heritage. 2007. *Major Archaeological Discoveries in China (in 2006)*. Beijing: Cultural Relics Press.

Christie, Agatha. 1936. *Murder in Mesopotamia*. William Collins.

——. 1946. *Come, Tell Me How You Live*. William Collins.

Clark, Peter (ed.). 2004. *The Dover Bronze Age Boat*. English Heritage.

Clarke, David L. 1968. *Analytical Archaeology*. London: Methuen.

Colardelle, Michel, and E. Verdelle. 1993. *Les habitats du lac de Paladru (Isère) dans leur environnement*. Paris: Editions de la Maison des Sciences e l'Homme.

Conyers, Lawrence B. 2010. Ground-penetrating radar for anthropological research. *Antiquity* 84: 175–184.

Cox, Margaret, and John Hunter. 2005. *Forensic Archaeology. Advances in Theory and Practice*. London and New York: Routledge.

Crone, Anne, and Ciara Clarke. 2005. A programme for wetland archaeology in Scotland in the 21st century. *Proceedings of the Society of Antiquaries of Scotland* 135: 5–17.

Crubézy, Eric et al. 2009. Tombes gelées de Siberie. In Jean Guilaine (ed.), *Sépultures et sociétés du Néolithique à l'histoire*, 313–333. Paris: Editions Errance.

Dalland, Magnar. 1984. A procedure for use in stratigraphic analysis. *Scottish Archaeological Review* 3.2: 116–127.

Deevy, Mary B., and Donald Murphy (eds.). 2009. *Places along the Way: First Findings on the M3.* NRA Scheme Monographs 5.

Denham, Tim, Simon Haberle, and Alain Pierret. 2009. A multi-disciplinary method for the investigation of early agriculture: Learning lessons from Kuk. In Fairbairn et al. 2009, 139–154.

Department for Communities and Local Government (UK). 2010. Planning Policy Statement 5: Planning for the Historic Environment. Retrieved from *www.tso.co.uk.*

Devereux, B. J., G. S. Amable, P. Crow, and A. D. Cliff. 2005. The potential of airborne radar for detection of archaeological features under woodland canopies. *Antiquity* 79: 648–660.

Dixon, Nicholas. 2004. *The Crannogs of Scotland. An Underwater Archaeology.* Stroud: Tempus.

Eddy, Frank W., Fred Wendorf, and associates. 1999. *An Archaeological Investigation of the Central Sinai, Egypt.* Boulder: University Press of Colorado.

English Heritage. 1997. *Conservation Plans: A Brief Introduction.* London.

——. 2006. *Conservation Principles.* London.

——. 2008. Management of Research Projects in the Historic Environment (MoRPHE). Retrieved from *http://www.english-heritage.org.uk/professional/.*

——. 2010. PPS5 Planning for the Historic Environment: Historic Environment Planning Practice Guide. Retrieved from *www.english-heritage.org.uk.*

Eun-Joo Lee, Dong Hoon Shin, Hoo Yul Yang, Mark Spigelman, and Se Gweon Yim. 2009. Eung Tae's tomb: A Joseon ancestor and the letters of those that loved him. *Antiquity* 83: 145–156.

Everill, Paul. 2009. *The Invisible Diggers. A Study of British Commercial Archaeology.* Oxford: Oxbow.

Evershed, R. P., and R. C. Connolly. 1988. Lipid preservation in Lindow Man. *Naturwissenschaften* 75: 143–145.

Evershed, R. P., C. Heron, and L. J. Goad. 1991. Epicuticular wax components preserved in potsherds as chemical indicators of leafy vegetables in ancient diets. *Antiquity* 65: 540–544.

Evershed, R. P., S. N. Dudd, M. J. Lockheart, and S. Jim. 2001. Lipids in archaeology. In Brothwell and Higgs 2001, 331–350.

169

Fairbairn, Andrew, Sue O'Connor, and Ben Marwick (eds.). 2009. *New Directions in Archaeological Science.* Terra Australis 28. Canberra: ANU E Press, Australian National University.

Fanning, Patricia, Simon Holdaway, and Rebecca Phillipps. 2009. Heat-retainer hearth identification as a component of archaeological survey in western NSW, Australia. In Fairbairn et al. 2009, 13–23.

FAS-Heritage Ltd. 2010. Conservation and Research Management Plan, Eilean Donan Castle Ross-shire. Client report.

Faßbinder J. W. E., and W. Irlinger. 1996. Luftbild und magnetische Prospektion zur Erforschung einer keltischen Viereckschanze bei Oberframmering. *Das archäologische Jahr in Bayern* 1995, 93–96.

Fourment, Nathalie. 2004. La comprehension des niveaux d'habitat en contexte stratifié: Problématique d'étude et développement d'analyses méthodologiques pour deux sites de la fin du Paléolitiques supérieur dans le sud de la France. In Geoff Carver (ed.), *Digging the Dirt. Excavation in the New Millennium*, 193–216. BAR International Series 1256.

Framework Archaeology. 2008. *From Hunter-Gatherers to Huntsmen. A History of the Stansted Landscape.* Framework Archaeology Monograph 2. Wessex Archaeological Reports.

Gaffney, C. 2008. Detecting trends in the prediction of the buried past: A review of geophysical techniques in archaeology. *Archaeometry* 50: 313–336.

Graves, Robert. 1960. *The Greek Myths I.* New York: Penguin.

Greatorex, R. 2004. Towards an integrated European recording system for archaeology: The problems that lie ahead. In Geoff Carver (ed.), *Digging the Dirt. Excavation in the New Millennium*, 265–268. BAR International Series 1256.

Grün, R. 2001. Trapped charge dating (ESR, TL, OSL). In Brothwell and Pollard (eds.) 2001, 47–62.

Hall, Allan, and Harry Kenward. 2003. Can we identify biological indicator groups for craft, industry and other activities? In P. Murphy and P. E. J. Wiltshire (eds.), *The Environmental Archaeology of Industry. Symposia of the Association for Environmental Archaeology* 20, 114–130. Oxford: Oxbow.

Hammond, Norman. 1991a. Matrices and Maya archaeology. *Journal of Field Archaeology* 18: 29–42.

——. (ed.). 1991b. *Cuello. An Early Maya Community in Belize.* Cambridge: Cambridge University Press.

Harris, E. C. 1975. The stratigraphic sequence: A question of time. *World Archaeology* 7.1: 109–121.

——. 1989. *Principles of Archaeological Stratigraphy*. 2nd edition. London and New York: Academic Press.

Harris, E. C., M. R. Brown III, and G. J. Brown (eds.). 1993. *Practices of Archaeological Stratigraphy*. New York: Academic Press.

Hawkes, J. 1982. *Mortimer Wheeler. Adventurer in Archaeology*. London: Weidenfeld and Nicholson.

Hebsgaard, M. B., M. T. P. Gilbert, J. Arneborg, P. Heyn, M. E. Allentoft, M. Bunce, K. Munch, C. Schweger, and E. Willeslev. 2009. The Farm beneath the Sand—An archaeological case study on ancient "dirt" DNA. *Antiquity* 83: 430–444.

Heffernan, Thomas. 1988. *Wood Quay. The Clash over Dublin's Past*. Austin: University of Texas Press.

Herries, Andy I. R. 2009. New approaches for integrating palaeomagnetic and mineral magnetic methods to answer archaeological and geological questions on Stone Age sites. In Fairbairn et al., 235–254.

Hester T. R., H. J. Shafer, and K. L. Feder. 1997. *Field Methods in Archaeology*. 7th edition. California: Mayfield Publishing.

Hey, Gill. 2006. Scale and archaeological evaluations: What are we looking for? In Gary Lock and Brian Leigh Molyneaux (eds.), *Confronting Scale in Archaeology. Issues of Theory and Practice*, 113–127. New York: Springer.

Hills, C. M. 1977. *The Anglo-Saxon Cemetery at Spong Hill, North Elmham, Norfolk*. Gressenhall.

Hirst, S. 1976. *Recording on Excavations I: The Written Record*. Hertfordshire: Rescue, The British Archaeological Trust.

Historic Scotland. 2003. *Preparation and Use of Lime Mortars*. Edinburgh.

——. 2009. Scottish Historic Environment Policy SHEP 2009. Retrieved from *http://www.historic-scotland.gov.uk/shep-july-2009.pdf*.

Hjulstro, B., and S. Isaksson. 2009. Identification of activity area signatures in a reconstructed Iron Age house by combining element and lipid analyses of sediments. *Journal of Archaeological Science* 36: 174–183.

HM Government (UK). 2010. The Government's Statement on the Historic Environment for England. Retrieved from *www.tso.co.uk*.

Hodder, Ian. 1997. Always momentary, fluid and flexible: Towards a reflexive excavation method. *Antiquity* 71: 691–700.

——. 1999. *The Archaeological Process*. Blackwell.

—— (ed.). 2005. *Inhabiting Çatalhöyük. Reports from the 1995–1999 Seasons*. Cambridge: British Institute of Archaeology at Ankara.

Hope-Taylor, Brian. 1977. *Yeavering: An Anglo-British Centre of Early Northumbria*. London: HMSO.

Howard A. J., A. G. Brown, C. J. Carey, K Challis, L. P. Cooper, M. Kincey, and P. Toms. 2008. Archaeological resource modelling in temperate river valleys: A case study from the Trent Valley, UK. *Antiquity* 82: 1040–1054.

Högberg, Anders, Kathryn Puseman, and Chad Yost. 2009. Integration of use-wear with protein residue analysis—A study of tool use and function in the south Scandinavian Early Neolithic. *Journal of Archaeological Science* 36.8: 1725–1737.

Hume, Ivor Noel. 1982. *Martin's Hundred*. London.

Jordan, D., 2009. How effective is geophysical survey? A regional review. *Archaeological Prospection* 16: 77–90.

Kenward, H. K. 1978. The analysis of archaeological insect assemblages: A new approach. *The Archaeology of York* 19.1. London: Council for British Archaeology.

Keys, Ben. 2009. Engrained in the past: Using geoarchaeology to understand site formation processes at the Gledswood Shelter 1 site, Northwest Queensland. BA dissertation, Flinders University, Australia.

Kidder, A. V. 1924 [2000]. *An Introductory Study of Southwestern Archaeology, with a Preliminary Account of the Excavation at Pecos*. Reissued with a new essay by Douglas W. Schwarz. New Haven: Yale University Press.

King, Thomas F. 2005. *Doing Archaeology. A Cultural Resource Management Perspective*. Walnut Creek, CA: Left Coast.

——. 2010. My Historic Environment. *The Historic Environment* 1.1: 103–104.

Kintigh, Keith. 2006. The promise and challenge of archaeological data integration. *American Antiquity* 71.3: 567–578.

Knowles, Elizabeth (ed.). 1999. *The Oxford Dictionary of Quotations*. Oxford.

Koldewey, Robert. 1914. *The Excavations at Babylon*. London: Macmillan.

Leckebusch J. 2003. Ground-penetrating radar: A modern three-dimensional prospection method. *Archaeological Prospection* 10: 213–240.

Liangren, Zhang. 2011. A new archaeology: China meets Soviet Russia. *Antiquity* 85: 1049–1059.

Linderholm, Anna, Charlotte Hedenstierna Jonson, Olle Svensk, and Kerstin Lidén. 2008. Diet and status in Birka: Stable isotopes and grave goods compared. *Antiquity* 82: 446–461.

Mallowan, Max. 1977 [reprint 2001]. *Mallowan's Memoirs*. New York: Harper Collins.

Matthews, W., C. A. I. French, T. Lawrence, D. Cuttler, and M. K. Jones. 1997. Microstratigraphic traces of site formation processes and human activities. *World Archaeology* 29.2: 281–308.

Matthews, Wendy. 2005. Micromorphological and microstratigraphic traces of uses and concepts of space. In Hodder 2005, 355–398.

McCoy, Mark, and Michael Graves. 2010. The role of agricultural innovation on Pacific Islands: A case study from Hawai'i Island. *World Archaeology* 42.1: 90–107.

McCullagh, R. P. J., and R. Tipping (eds.). 1998. *The Lairg Project 1988–1996. The Evolution of an Archaeological Landscape in Northern Scotland.* Monograph 3. Edinburgh: Scottish Trust for Archaeological Research.

Mercer, Roger, and Magdelana S. Midgley. 1997. The early Bronze Age cairn at Sketewan, Balnaguard, Perth and Kinross. *Proceedings of the Society of Antiquaries of Scotland* 127: 281–338.

Middleton, William D., T. Douglas Price, and David Meiggs. 2005. Chemical analysis of floor sediments for the identification of anthropogenic activity residues. In Hodder 2005, 399–412.

Milek, Karen B. 2006. Houses and households in early Icelandic Society: Geoarchaeology and the interpretation of social space. Unpublished PhD dissertation, University of Cambridge.

Müldner, Gundula et al. 2009. Isotopes and individuals: Diet and mobility among the medieval bishops of Whithorn. *Antiquity* 83: 1119–1133.

Müller-Wille, Michael (ed.). 1991. *Starigrad/Oldenburg. Ein slawischer Herrschersitz, des frühen Mittelalters in Ostholstein.* Neumünster: Karl Wach-holtz.

National Roads Authority (NRA). 2005. *The M3 Clonee to North of Kells Motorway*. Archaeology Information Series. NRA and Meath County Council.

Neumann, Thomas W., and Robert M. Sanford. 2001. *Cultural Resources Archaeology. An Introduction.* Walnut Creek, CA: AltaMira Press.

Novembre, John, Toby Johnson, Katarzyna Bryc, Zoltán Kutalik, Adam R. Boyko, Adam Auton, Amit Indap, Karen S. King, Sven Bergmann, Matthew R. Nelson, Matthew Stephens, and Carlos D. Bustamante. 2008. Genes mirror geography within Europe. *Nature*, November 6; 456 (7218): 98–101.

Odell, George H. 2001. Research Problems R Us. *American Antiquity* 66.4: 679–685.

Ogalde, Juan P., Bernardo T. Arriaza, and Elia C. Soto. 2009. Identification of psychoactive alkaloids in ancient Andean human hair by gas chromatography/mass spectrometry. *Journal of Archaeological Science* 36.2: 467–472.

Oonk, S., C. P. Slomp, D .J. Huisman, and S. P. Vriend. 2009. Effects of site lithology on geochemical signatures of human occupation in archaeological house plans in the Netherlands. *Journal of Archaeological Science* 36.6: 1215–1228.

O'Hara, Robert. 2009. Early Medieval settlement at Roestown 2. In Mary B. Deevy and Donald Murphy (eds.), *Places along the Way. First Findings on the M3*, 57–82. NRA Scheme Monographs 5.

O'Sullivan, Aidan. 2001. *Foragers, Farmer and Fishers in a Coastal Landscape. An Intertidal Archaeological Survey of the Shannon Estuary*. Discovery Programme Monograph 5.

O'Sullivan, Jerry. 1999. Iona: Archaeological investigations, 1875–1996. In Dauvit Broun and Thomas Owen Clancy (eds.), *Spes Scotorum*, 215–244. Edinburgh: T&T Clark.

Paice, P. 1991. Extensions to the Harris matrix system to illustrate stratigraphic discussion of an archaeological site. *Journal of Field Archaeology* 18: 17–28.

Payne, S. 1972. Partial recovery and sample bias. The results of some sieving experiments. In E. S. Higgs (ed.), *Papers in Economic Prehistory*, 49–64. Cambridge.

Petrie, Flinders. 1904. *Methods and Aims in Archaeology*. London: Methuen.

Phillips, Tim, and Richard Bradley. 2004. Developer-funded fieldwork in Scotland, 1990–2003: An overview of the prehistoric evidence. *Proceedings of the Society of Antiquaries of Scotland* 134: 17–51.

Piggott, Stuart. 1965. *Ancient Europe from the Beginnings of Agriculture to Classical Antiquity*. Edinburgh University Press.

Pitt-Rivers A. L. F. 1886–90. *Excavations in Cranborne Chase*. 4 vols. Privately printed.

Pitts, Mike. 2009. A year at Stonehenge. *Antiquity* 83: 184–194.

Pitulko, V. V. 2007. Methods of excavating Stone Age sites associated with permafrost. *Archaeology, Enthology and Anthropology of Eurasia* 31.3: 29–38.

———. 2008. Principal excavations techniques under permafrost conditions (based on Zhokhov and Yana Sites, Northern Yakutia). *Archaeology, Enthology and Anthropology of Eurasia* 34.2: 26–33.

Pruvost, Mélanie, Reinhard Schwarz, Virginia Bessa Correia, Sophie Champlot, Séverine Braguier, Nicolas Morel, Yolanda Fernandez-Jalvo, Thierry Grange, and Eva-Maria Geigl. 2007. Freshly excavated fossil bones are best for amplification of ancient DNA. *Proceedings of the National Academy of Sciences* 104.3: 739–744.

Ramqvist, Per. 1992. *Högöm. The Excavations of 1949–1984.* Umeå.

Ravesloot, John C., and Michael R. Waters. 2004. Geoarchaeology and archaeological site patterning on the middle Gila River, Arizona. *Journal of Field Archaeology* 29.1/2: 203–214.

Redman C. 1973. Multi-stage fieldwork and analytical techniques. *American Antiquity* 38: 61–79.

———. 1987. Surface collection, sampling and research design: A retrospective. *American Antiquity* 52.2: 249–265.

Reinecke, Andreas, Vin Laychour, and Seng Sonetra. 2009. *The First Golden Age of Cambodia: Excavation at Prohear.* German Foreign Office.

Renfrew, Colin. 2007. *Excavations at Phylakopi in Melos 1974–77.* British School at Athens.

Rhodes, Edward J., Patricia Fanning, Simon Holdaway, and Cynthja Bolton. 2009. Archaeological surfaces in western NSW: Stratigraphic contexts and preliminary OSL dating of hearths. In Fairbairn et al. 2009, 189–199.

Rich, Claudius J. 1816. *Memoir on the Ruins of Babylon.* London: Longman.

Roskams, Steve. 2001. *Excavation.* Cambridge Manuals in Archaeology. Cambridge.

Sabloff, Jeremy A. 2008. *Archaeology Matters. Action Archaeology in the Modern World.* Walnut Creek, CA: Left Coast.

Saiano, F., and R. Scalenghe. 2009. An anthropic soil transformation fingerprinted by REY patterns. *Journal of Archaeological Science* 36.11: 2502–2506.

Saunders, Tom. 2004. Breaking up time: The problems of "phasing stratigraphy." In Geoff Carver (ed.), *Digging the Dirt. Excavation in the New Millennium,* 163–171. BAR International Series 1256.

Scheiber, Laura L., and Judson Byrd Finley. 2010. Domestic campsites and cyber landscapes in the Rocky Mountains. *Antiquity* 84: 114–130.

Schiffer, Michael. 1976. *Behavioral Archaeology*. New York: Academic Press.

——. 1987. *Formation Processes of the Archaeological Record*. Albuquerque: University of New Mexico Press.

Sealy, J. 2001. Body tissue chemistry and palaeodiet. In Brothwell and Pollard 2001, 269–299.

Seymour, D. J. 2009. Nineteenth-century Apache wickiups: Historically documented models for archaeological signatures of the dwellings of mobile people. *Antiquity* 83: 157–165.

Sharer, Robert J., and Wendy Ashmore. 1979. *Fundamentals of Archaeology*. London: Benjamin/Cummings.

Sherwood, Sarah, Boyce N. Driskell, Asa R. Randall, and Scott C. Meeks. 2004. Chronology and stratigraphy at Dust Cave, Alabama. *American Antiquity* 69: 533–554.

Skibo, James M. Michael W. Graves, and Miriam T. Stark (eds.). 2007. *Archaeological Anthropology. Perspectives on Method and Theory*. Tucson: University of Arizona Press.

Smith, Colin I., Andrew T. Chamberlain, Michael S. Riley, Chris Stringer, and Matthew J. Collins. 2003. The thermal history of human fossils and the likelihood of successful DNA amplification. *Journal of Human Evolution* 45: 203–217.

Smith, Helen, P. Marshall, and M. Parker Pearson. 2001. Reconstructing house activity areas. In U. Albarella (ed.), *Environmental Archaeology: Meaning and Purpose*, 249–270. Dordrecht: Kluwer.

Streuver, S. 1968. Flotation techniques for the recovery of small scale archaeological remains. *American Antiquity* 33: 353–362.

Stuart-Williams, H. le Q., H. P. Schwarcz, C. D. White, and M.W. Spence. 1996. The isotopic composition and diagenesis of human bone from Teotihuacan and Oaxaca, Mexico. *Palaeogeography, Palaeoclimatology, Palaeoecology* 126: 1–14.

Swedish National Heritage Board. 2006. Towards Future Heritage Management. The Swedish National Heritage Board's Environmental Scanning Report. Retrieved from *http://www.raa.se/cms/showdocument/ documents/extern_webbplats/2007/juni/9789172094581.pdf*.

Trinks, I., J. Nissen, B. Johansson, J. Emilsson, C. Gustafsson, J. Friborg, and J. Gustafsson. 2008. Pilot study of the new multichannel GPR system MIRA for large scale, high resolution archaeological prospection at the site of the Viking town Birka in Sweden. *Newsletter of the International Society for Archaeological Prospection* 16: 4–7.

Trinks, I., J. Gustafsson, J. Emilsson, J. Friborg, C. Gustafsson, B. Johansson, and J. Nissen. 2009. Efficient, large-scale archeological prospection using a true 3D GPR array. In D. Marguerie and P. Lanos (eds.), *Mémoire du sol, espace des hommes*, 367–370. Rennes: Presses Universitaires de Rennes.

Tryon, Christian A. 2006. The destructive potential of earthworms on the archaeobotanical record. *Journal of Field Archaeology* 31.2: 199–202.

University College Dublin. 2006. *Archaeology 2020: Repositioning Irish Archaeology in the Knowledge Society. A Realistically Achievable Perspective.* University College Dublin and The Heritage Council. Retrieved from *www.ucd.ie/archaeology.*

Van de Velde, Pieter (ed.). 2007. *Excavations at Geleen-Janskamperveld 1990/1991.* Analecta Praehistorica Leidensia 39.

Vanzetti A., M. Vidale, M. Gallinaro, D.W. Frayer, and L. Bondioli. 2010. The Ice Man as a burial. *Antiquity* 84: 681–692.

Verhagen, Philip, and Arno Borsboom. 2009. The design of effective and efficient trial trenching strategies for discovering archaeological sites. *Journal of Archaeological Science* 36.8: 1807–1815.

Vitousek, P. M., T. N. Ladefoged, P. V. Kirch, A. S. Hartshorn, M. W. Graves, S. C. Hotchkiss, S. Tuljapurkar, and O. A. Chadwick. 2004. Soils, agriculture, and society in precontact Hawai'i. *Science* 304: 1165–1169.

Watson, Bruce. 2004. From mud to monograph. In Geoff Carver (ed.), *Digging the Dirt. Excavation in the New Millennium,* 75–78. BAR International Series 1256.

Watson, Patty Jo. 1969. *The Prehistory of Salts Cave, Kentucky.* Illinois State Museum, Reports of Investigations 16.

—— (ed.). 1997. *Archeology of the Mammoth Cave Area.* St. Louis: Cave Books.

Wendorf, Fred, and Raymond H. Thompson. 2002. The Committee for the Recovery of Archaeological Remains: Three decades of service to the archaeological profession. *American Antiquity* 67.2: 317–330.

Wheeler, R.E.M. 1943. *Maiden Castle, Dorset.* London: Society of Antiquaries Research Report 12.

——. 1954. *Archaeology from the Earth*. Oxford: Clarendon Press.

——. 1956. *Still Digging*. London: Michael Joseph.

——. 1968. Review of Hod Hill 2. *Antiquity* 42: 149–150.

Willey, Gordon R. (ed.). 1953. *Prehistoric Settlement Patterns in the Virú Valley, Peru*. Bureau of American Ethnology Bulletin 155. Washington, DC: Smithsonian Institute.

——. 1999. The Virú Valley projects and settlement archaeology: Some reminiscences and contemporary comments. In Brian R. Billman and Gary M. Feinman (eds.), *Settlement Pattern Studies in the Americas. Fifty Years since Virú*, 9–11. Washington and London: Smithsonian Institution Press.

Wilson, Claire A, Donald A. Davidson and Malcolm S Cresser. 2008. Multi-element soil analysis: An assessment of its potential as an aid to archaeological interpretation. *Journal of Archaeological Science* 35.2: 412–424.

Woolley, Leonard. 1920. *Dead Towns and Living Men*. Oxford.

# INDEX

# ABOUT THE AUTHOR

Martin Carver is Emeritus Professor of Archaeology at the University of York, editor of the journal *Antiquity*, and the author of *Archaeological Investigation* (Routledge, 2009). He has undertaken or advised on field projects in England, Scotland, Sweden, France, Italy, and Algeria, including numerous commercial projects and major research campaigns at Sutton Hoo and Portmahomack.